Elizabeth Williams Champney

Three Vassar Girls on the Rhine

A Holiday Trip of Three College Girls Through Germany

Elizabeth Williams Champney

Three Vassar Girls on the Rhine
A Holiday Trip of Three College Girls Through Germany

ISBN/EAN: 9783744760218

Printed in Europe, USA, Canada, Australia, Japan

Cover: Foto ©Thomas Meinert / pixelio.de

More available books at **www.hansebooks.com**

THREE VASSAR GIRLS

On the Rhine.

A HOLIDAY TRIP OF THREE COLLEGE GIRLS THROUGH
GERMANY, BY WAY OF THIS CELEBRATED
RIVER.

LIZZIE W. CHAMPNEY.

ILLUSTRATED BY "CHAMP"
AND OTHERS.

BOSTON:
ESTES AND LAURIAT, PUBLISHERS.
1887.

CONTENTS.

ILLUSTRATIONS.

THREE VASSAR GIRLS ON THE RHINE.

THREE VASSAR GIRLS ON THE RHINE.

CHAPTER I.

DELIGHT HOLMES' JOURNAL.

ANTWERP, July.

GOOD-BYE.

IT was a great disappointment to me that my father and mother could not make this trip to Europe with me.

The greater part of my pleasure during our delightful South American journey was due to their presence, and I do not think that I could have borne to have seen father's figure grow more indistinct as he waved his farewell to me from the dock, and the steamer carried me out into the fog, if the tour had been for pleasure alone. But the prospect of travelling with my dear friend Myrtle, and of settling down for a year at a German University town to the study of difficult botany and microscopy, opened such vistas before me of future opportunities as a naturalist, that I yielded to mother's urging, and here I am.

I foresee that I shall find a great deal of enjoyment in this journal. I shall feel that I am sharing my pleasures with my parents, since it is to be sent to them, and that I am coming to them for advice, though I shall be hardly able to receive their counsel before the occasion for which I need it shall have passed.

And first I must describe my travelling companions, and I will try to do so in a manner becoming the daughter of a scientist. I remember that father said that a naturalist must be a close observer, and I recall how he sat for three hours watching the habits of a spider. If I am to analyze plants and note their affinities, it will certainly be good practice to begin by analyzing people and assigning them to their different genera and species.

My friend Myrtle has too simple and homely a name; she is more like some glorious tropical flower. She is a Southern girl, and her father is Colonel Boujoulac, noted, they say, during the last war, as the dashing commander of the "Louisiana Tigers." He was wounded in that desperate assault during the second day's fight at Gettysburg. There is nothing ferocious about him now, however; he is president of a railroad, and has a lazy but perfectly gentlemanly manner, as though every pursuit but that of playing cards were too laborious an exertion to be thought of.

During our college days, Myrtle was a special student, paying particular attention to modern languages and music. My best friend, Victoria, did not greatly care for her, though I loved her

COL. BOUJOULAC.

dearly. It has been said that triangular friendships are hard to manage. Affection cannot be distributed between three people in just the same measure.

While Victoria went with us to South America, Myrtle was hanging over her mother's sick-bed. I think the death of Mrs. Boujoulac has made a great change in Myrtle, and that she is now filled with the noble ambition of being everything to her father. Victoria is so full of energy herself, and has accomplished so much since g.

graduation, in the study of medicine in Zurich, and its practice among the poor cholera-smitten people of Naples, that Myrtle suffers in comparison, but I cannot help thinking that there are grand possibilities in Myrtle. I remember that, when this tour was first mentioned, she said she felt her father needed it. I thought at the time that perhaps he had fallen into melancholy since his wife's death, or that he was out of health; he seems, however, very well, and even gay, and I cannot quite account for the anxious look which Myrtle occasionally gives

MYRTLE.

him. Two girls could not differ more than Myrtle Boujoulac and I. She is fascinating, brave, and extravagantly generous. I am insignificant, and have only one talent, my father's, for work. I am what the college slang calls "a regular dig." Myrtle, though scarcely a year my senior, looks a woman; she dresses always elegantly. Whether in many-ruffled white muslins, or fashionable close-fitting costumes, there is always a certain touch of style which is more than that given by the dressmaker. Some one has said that she could make any dress fashionable by wearing it, while I am always the same commonplace individual in the prettiest costume. I confess, however, that I do not like to study effects of dress.

DELIGHT.

My travelling suit is a cloth jacket, with pleated skirt, hair drawn back, and a Scotch cap. I shall be comfortable, but not

After a glimpse at the Netherlands we expect to be joined at Cologne by a Miss Boylston, also a Vassar graduate, and a friend to my friend Maud Van Vechten. One good thing about Vassar friendships is that they make a chain of good fellowship extending all around the world. Maud passes me on to this friend of hers, whom I have never seen, but who is sure to be kind to me for Maud's and Vassar's sake, and who will be very useful to us, for she has been studying music in different parts of Germany for the past three or four years. We have another friend waiting our arrival, in Myrtle's brother Joe, who is a student at the University of Bonn.

We left New York the 30th of June, on the Red Star steamer "—— land," bound for Antwerp. I think we were first attracted to this steamer by a set of decorations in the cabin, made by a company of artists which crossed upon it one season. We had no reason to regret our choice, for these paintings were a source of continual comfort and inspiration to us. In the stormy weather, which pursued us nearly all the way across the Atlantic, we were obliged to keep the cabin and devote ourselves, — Myrtle to Kensington embroidery, and I to Motley's "Rise of the Dutch Republic." I began by reading aloud all the interesting passages, and finished by becoming the centre of a little group of ladies, and by reading every bit to them, and the "United Netherlands" as well. It was a good preparation for what we were to see of Belgium and Holland before beginning our voyage up the classic river Rhine, and the sketches about us gave rein to the imagination, for they were chiefly foretastes of what we were to see; heads of peasants, windmills, and spires of distant cathedrals. There was one ruined castle of which Myrtle was particularly fond. It seemed familiar to her, as though she had seen it in a dream, she said, or lived in it in some previous state of existence "I am sure that it is connected with my fate in some way," she 'ith say. "Something remarkable either has happened or will hap. was me there." I pooh-poohed the notion. "You have seen a phot,g.

of it somewhere," I explained, " and the memory haunts you. Either
that is it, or it strikes your fancy as what a Rhine castle ought to be.
Ruins are very conventional; they all hold to a general fashion, a
dungeon-keep half overgrown with ivy, a few cart-loads of rubbish at
the foot, a grass-grown moat, a liberal supply of moonlight, and a
trifle of river, and there you are."

I delivered this recipe for a castle very confidently, for I had never
seen one, — and one's assurance about anything is generally in exact
proportion to one's ignorance. My raillery made no impression upon
Myrtle; she continued to regard her castle with a pensive air, which
was almost depressing. It did not occur to me at the time that she
had some other cause for melancholy which was hiding itself in this
picturesque ruin. I noticed that each morning she invited her father
to listen to the reading. Sometimes he lingered for a few moments,
but after a time he was sure to finger
his cigar-case, and soon after he
would beat a precipitate retreat for
the smoking-room. When we went
on deck for our constitutional just before lunch, we would see him playing
innumerable games of poker with
other gentlemen of like tastes. His
partner was usually a dark Jewish-
looking man, for whom Myrtle had
contracted a strong antipathy, though
he was perfectly polite and gentlemanly, both in his behavior to her,

MR. VAN BERGEN.

and, as far as I could judge, to every one. He professes to be a diamond-cutter from Amsterdam. He came to America on business
.... ected with the diamond exhibit made at the Centennial, and was
y tr ,much pleased with our country that this is his first return trip to
.s native country. He gave his name as Solomon Van Bergen, and

said that he was a descendant of Louis Van Berguen of Bruges, who discovered the art of cutting diamonds, in the fifteenth century. One evening the chat turned upon precious stones, and Colonel Boujoulac asked Myrtle to show her mother's diamond cross. I shall never forget the expression of Mr. Van Bergen's face when the jewels were laid in his hand; admiration, greed, and a malicious cunning seemed united in that first glance. When he spoke, however, it was only to disparage the stones, which he said were not of the first water, though it would improve them greatly to be reset, as the clumsy old silver settings were not calculated to show off their lustre. He offered to direct Colonel Boujoulac to a responsible house where they could be remounted, and that gentleman seemed inclined to consider his offer; but Myrtle expressed herself afterwards as violently opposed to having them touched. I think she suspected Mr. Van Bergen of designs upon her diamonds, and that her dislike for the man dated from the look which he gave the cross when it first flashed upon him from its worn morocco case. Be this as it may, we bade good-bye to the diamond-cutter when the ship touched at Antwerp, and are not likely to meet him again, for he has gone directly on to Amsterdam, and we are loitering in this strange old town. As we steamed up the river Scheldt, lined with shipping, we were reminded of the almost fabulous stories told of Dutch commerce in the days of Charles V., when two thousand five hundred ships could be counted at one time upon the river, bound to and from Arabia, Persia, India, Africa, and all parts of the then civilized globe. A little country, like England, the Netherlands spread itself, in its colonies and trading-posts, in the East and West Indies, and in North and South America. How much of sturdy healthfulness we owe the Dutch stock. The aristocratic names of New York and Albany, and many excellent Dutch characteristics in our own people, are our inheritance from this enterprising and thrifty nation.

What though the discoveries and settlements of the Dutch

DUTCH TRADERS AT MANHATTAN.

made by the spirit of trade rather than that of adventure or conquest. These honest merchants, in their peaceable, prosaic lives, are more to be honored than the robbers and murderers of more glorious name, whose deeds are notorious in history. I for one am proud of our Dutch ancestry, and think the wealth and comfort attained by quiet industry by no means to be despised.

We found at the hotel a letter from Myrtle's brother Joe, introducing a friend, a certain Max Blumenthal, a young German, now studying art at the Antwerp Academy, who presently called upon us and took us to see the cathedral, which is one of the most beautiful in Europe. It has a Gothic spire four hundred feet high, covered with lace-like carving, and a magnificent chime of ninety-nine bells. It is said that the smallest bell is only fifteen inches in diameter, while the largest weighs eight tons. Mr. Blumenthal, who has lived for several years under the shadow of the cathedral spire, seems to love it as though it were a human being. He speaks English well for a German who has never been in England or America, and he gave us many interesting details in regard to the history of the cathedral. He says that in the 16th century it was far more beautiful than now. Then it boasted many sculptured saints in niches ornamented with intricate tracery of fruit, and flower, and beasts, and griffins, with effigies of crusaders in their armor, and gorgeous stained-glass windows. The banners of the nobility were suspended from the roof, and the altars blazed with gold and silver, but in 1564 occurred the revolt of the Gueux, or the Beggars. The rabble were at work everywhere, climbing over the altars, throwing down the images, mutilating and breaking them, and treading them under foot. Shoes were greased with the sacred oil, the windows were shattered, and havoc and ruin reigned.

"It almost makes me to be angry with the Protestant religion," Max Blumenthal said, "when I remember to myself what art has lost through those crazy fellows."

"They were crazed indeed," Myrtle replied; "but when you think of the cause, of the atrocities of the inquisition which Philip of Spain had established here, and of which these images were the representatives, I think we can but admire the principle of religious liberty which lay behind the mad deeds of the Iconoclasts or Image-breakers."

The young man listened gravely. "You are *properly* right" (he meant probably), he said. "You have made me to think of it in a new light. I find I look too much at the outside of things; I need some one to teach me what they shall all mean. Still, it was a pity to break those so glorious windows. I could not have persuaded with myself to do it."

"Yes, it was a pity," Myrtle admitted, "but nearly every reform is ushered in by a convulsion; and if it had not been for the determined spirit of the Netherlanders, Protestantism would have been extinguished."

He led us to the great picture of the cathedral, one of the great

RUBENS' "DESCENT FROM THE CROSS,"
IN ANTWERP CATHEDRAL.

ICONOCLASTS.

paintings of Europe — the " Descent from the Cross," by Rubens. It has been called " the grandest picture in the world, for composition, drawing, and coloring." We stood before it for some time in a sort

RUBENS.

of painful trance, it was so terribly life-like, the disciples and women so absorbed in their sad task. The white sheet into which the body is being lowered seemed to shed a reflected light across the anxious, sorrowful faces, and the pallid features of the murdered Christ. Myrtle, below her breath, repeated the lines, —

> " ' Remit the anguish of that lighted stare ;
> Close those wan lips ! let that thorn-wounded brow
> Stream not with blood.' "

Mr. Blumenthal told us of the two peasants who paused before the picture, one remaining entranced so long that the other pulled him along. " Hush! " replied the first, " *wait till they get him down.*"

Mr. Blumenthal is an enthusiastic admirer of Rubens, and in the afternoon we went with him to the Museum or Picture Gallery, to see other masterpieces by this celebrated painter. Certainly he was a great colorist, but I do not admire the type of women which he loved to represent. He was twice married; his first wife was Isabella Brant, and his second, Helena Formann. He painted them so often that it is said that the face of no painter's wife is so familiar to the world as are the faces of these two women. They were both fair, obese beauties, buxom and kindly, but unintellectual and gross. Rubens was one of the few artists who was splendidly successful during his lifetime. His genius was fully recognized by his contemporaries; he was rich and honored, and was several times sent upon diplomatic embassies to foreign countries. He is identified closely with Antwerp, though he was born in Westphalia, in 1577, and lived much in Italy, in Spain, and in France, where he left the wonderful pictures painted for Marie de Medicis. He was a handsome man, and the courtier's dress became him, " the great flapping hat, slightly cocked to one side," and the lace collar worn over sumptuous velvet. What would have been dandyism in a lesser man, was redeemed by his genius; we would not wish to imagine Rubens in modern dress, and, on the other hand, I think there are few 19th century men who could wear such a costume as he wore.

The Antwerp Gallery is rich, not only in paintings by Rubens, but also in Van Dycks. Van Dyck was born in Antwerp, and was a pupil of Rubens, but most of his portraits are in England, where he was court painter for Charles I.

A REALIST, FROM COUTURE.

We were much interested in the student life at the old Art Academy of Antwerp. The building was long ago a monastery, and its dreary corridors are paved with the monumental stones of the pious departed, and are to-day lightly trodden under foot by the careless students. I was surprised to learn that there are as many as fifteen hundred following the various branches of art instruction. Mr. Blumenthal said it was rare to find in Antwerp a person who, during some part of his life, had not attended the Academy; a greater part of the students, however, do not advance beyond the copying department.

"The Academy," he explained in his odd, foreign English, "does not undertake to make to be artists of its students, but only to teach them sometime to draw. Most of the fellows are realists, studying the form and the color for themselve simply, and justly as much interested in the still life — a cabbage, a handful of onions, or a head of swine — as in the most beautiful creation of the antique. Composition shall be studied later, and the imagination will have full play by and by, but at present we are learning the A B C of art."

Many of the most distinguished artists of the age, both in our own country and in England, have studied here, and the first prizes have been frequently carried off by Americans. It is a pity that women are not admitted, as at The Hague, where Vassar girls have won honor.

We shall see more of Antwerp and of Mr. Blumenthal later on, but Colonel Boujoulac wishes us to make a few excursions in Belgium before leaving for Holland and the Rhine; so to-morrow we leave for a short visit at Mechlin and Brussels.

CHAPTER II.

POINT LACE.

SWEEPING THE STREETS.

I HAVE said nothing of the architecture of the Netherlands, the quaint old houses with stepped gables, as though the weather-cocks were fond of going up and down stairs, the toppling appearance of the fronts owing to upper stories being built out a little beyond the lower, the numerous small-paned windows, and the extreme neatness everywhere. They say that Holland is cleaner still, but I do not see how that can be possible. We left Antwerp in the early morning, and the women were out busily sweeping the streets, a kind of broom-drill which would not be popular at home.

Mechlin is only fourteen miles from Antwerp, and the journey was quickly made. We spent the morning looking about the city.

Myrtle has an amateur photographic outfit which we unpacked at Antwerp, and are having great sport in using. It is instantaneous in its action, and we take people moving about, talking, gesticulating, as easily as when posed for a portrait. It is all boxed up in a neat little case, which has a very innocent look. We touch a spring, and we have a portrait without once exciting the subject's suspicions. While waiting for luncheon, we took an old gentleman deeply engaged in reading a book, and several passers on the street, some in wooden

THE BOOKWORM.

shoes, Brabant peasants, the old women with fine lace caps, with long ear-tabs, giving them the appearance of rabbits. Myrtle bought one of these caps in a store, it was so odd and picturesque. We saw some of the famous Mechlin lace, said to be the prettiest and lightest in the world, but we were told that it is no longer so fashionable as when Queen Elizabeth had her ruffs made of Mechlin, and Charles I. his falling collars. It is a pillow lace, made by winding bobbins of thread around needles set in the pillow in the required pattern; it is simple and not so expensive as Brussels lace, which has usurped its place. Myrtle liked it so much that she bought a large piece and generously gave half to me. The shop-girl kept assuring us that it was *snaeperig* and *doddrig*. I have heard these words so often from Dutch girls, that I am positive they mean "lovely" and "too sweet for anything," but I am not quite sure which is which. I am confirmed in my belief about these expressions, for I remember hearing one of the art students at the gallery say to a friend that Myrtle was a "snaeperig maedel mit een doddrig gesichtye." Maedel I know means girl, and gesichtye face. I feel as if I was becoming quite an adept in the language.

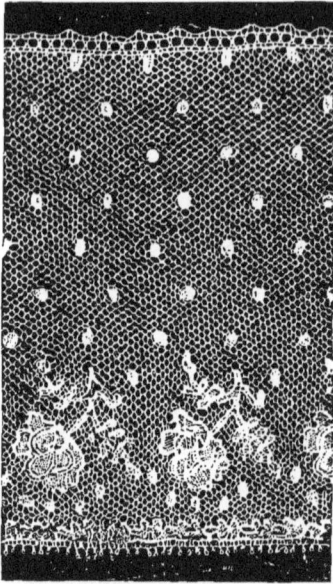

We saw some lace bleaching in the little shopkeeper's yard. The Colonel was looking at it thoughtfully, and I asked him of what he was thinking. He started. "It was preaching me a little sermon," he said.

"'The stained web which whitens in the sun
Grows pure by being purely shone upon.'

I was thinking of those lines, and of how very good I am becoming in the society of two such angelic young beings as yourself and my daughter."

His words were light, but I am sure

MECHLIN LACE.

that there was real feeling there at first. The Colonel seems to me more than ever attentive and indulgent to Myrtle, and I think that she is heartily glad that there is no Mr. Van Bergen here to wile him away to endless games of poker.

We found Mechlin so dull and sleepy that we took the afternoon train to Brussels, where there was far more to interest us. First, the beautiful Hotel de Ville, with its forty-windowed front, without counting the eighty dormers. We entered the historic States Chamber, with its old portraits and tapestry, a room in which it is mistakenly said Charles V. abdicted in favor of his son, Philip II. Motley says of the building, "Nearly in the heart of the city rose the audacious and exquisitely embroidered tower of the town-house, a miracle of needlework in stone, rivalling in its intricate carving the cobweb

HOTEL DE VILLE, BRUSSELS.

tracery of that lace which has for centuries been synonymous with
the city, and rearing itself above a façade of profusely decorated and
brocaded architecture."

It was in the Grand Place of Brussels, before the Hotel de Ville, that on the 5th of June, 1568, Counts Egmont and Horn were executed by the orders of the cruel Duke of Alva, and his master Philip II.

One feature peculiar to Brussels is the placing of little clocks at the street corners. We found this very convenient. Myrtle, who possesses a woman's fondness for shopping, was warned by one of these clocks that we were spending too much time in this spot of gloomy memories, and dragged me away in her search for a lace fichu. There are a hundred and forty establishments in the city for the manufacture of lace, so that our choice was a wide one. Luckily, Myrtle was able to content herself after a visit to five. Many of the pieces shown us were real works of art. We were told that the thread is made from Brabant flax, and is spun underground, for it is of such wonderful fineness that the least breath of wind will break it. We were given magnifying glasses, through which to view the lace, for some of the meshes were so delicate as to try the strongest eyesight. Brussels lace is not made all in one piece, but is composed of hundreds of bits, some worked by the needle and others on the pillow, and united by an invisible stitch. The flowers are often "applied," and the borders are especially rich and beautiful. The lady in charge told us that as many as sixty different hands had been employed on one scarf which she showed us, but that the general design was known only to one person. Myrtle's fingers gloated over this exquisite piece of work. "What is the price?" she asked in a quiet way, which seemed to say, "No matter what it is, I *must* have it."

"Two hondert and feefty dollars, madame. I do assure you it is ferry sheep."

"I will take it," Myrtle replied, calmly.

The Colonel whistled. "Isn't that rather extravagant?" he asked.

" But, papa," Myrtle replied, " I certainly have something for the money, while the three hundred you lost to Mr. Van Bergen gave you nothing but the satisfaction of having been beaten in playing your favorite game."

The Colonel elevated his eyebrows and paid for the scarf without further parley. It is the first time that Myrtle has made any allusion

BRUSSELS LACE.

to this subject, and I never suspected that the Colonel played for money. Is it possible that my dear friend's father is a *gambler?* I cannot believe it. It is a terrible weakness, a disease to which he is subject, and it accounts for Myrtle's anxiety and melancholy. How will it all end?

LATER.

Last evening we spent at the Weirtz Gallery, a collection of paintings by an eccentric painter; many of these are " trompes-l'œil," or deceptions, so cleverly managed that, although you are expecting them, you are sure to be deceived. For instance, while you are walking soberly along looking at the pictures which purport to be pictures, you pass a half-open door; curiosity invariably makes you give a glance over your shoulder as you go by, and in the adjoining apartment you are shocked to see some one dressing. You turn by an impulse of charity to close the door, and find that what you had taken for a view into another room is only a clever painting. Some of the pictures, notably the visions of a condemned man, a suicide, and the awakening of a man buried alive, are startling in the extreme. The painter had a genius beyond trickery, as well as for it.

We did not neglect the cathedral of Brussels with its magnificent façade and its beautiful interior, whose most notable objects are twelve splendid statues of the apostles, and the pulpit, the finest piece of wood-carving I ever saw. It represents Adam and Eve driven from Paradise. The figures support a globe in which the preacher stands.

After a night's rest, we set out early this morning for a drive to the battle-field of Waterloo, by way of the Forest of Soignies, to the village of Mont St. Jean, where a mound has been raised, on which stands the Lion of Waterloo. This colossal beast was cast from cannon taken from the French. From its base a fine view is obtained of the battle-field in which the "Iron Duke" crushed the first Napoleon. A little boy came up to us and tried to sell us some relics, buttons and bits of cloth. Colonel Boujoulae looked at them reflectively and gave the boy a coin, but declined to take his wares. "I suppose some day that pedlers at Gettysburg will be hawking the bones of my comrades," he said, sadly.

"I do not think you need waste any sentiment, papa," Myrtle remarked; "I am sure that these are manufactured relics, of a much later date than 1815."

Guide-book in hand, we followed the Colonel from one farm-

WATERLOO.

house to another, striving to understand the topography of this most famous and decisive battle of modern times.

"If I had had 'the Tigers' here, Napoleon need not have given in," said the Colonel; "we had a great deal harder row to hoe at Breed's Hill," and then we went over the different positions of Marshal Ney and Blücher. The enthusiasm of the old campaigner kindled at the famous reply of the Old Guard to Wellington's de-

RUIN OF HOUGOMONT.

mand of surrender as he saw it being annihilated. "The Guard dies, but never surrenders."

We walked through the park and about the ruins of the château of Hougomont, where nearly six thousand men were killed, and were shown the spot where the fires were extinguished just at the feet of a little image of the Virgin. To me it all seemed very sad, and I am sure that no nation ought to call itself civilized as long as war exists; but the Colonel was in his element, and declared that this was the most enjoyable day he had spent on European soil.

As we rode back toward Brussels, we were all a little silent, Myrtle and I from exhaustion, but the Colonel was thinking deeply. The sun had set, and twilight was drawing its veil across the landscape, when he spoke: —

"Myrtle," he said, "we have each our Waterloo to fight; mine is my love of gaming, yours is our family trait, extravagance. I have something serious to say, and I am quite willing that your friend should hear it. It startles me to see you spend money as you did yesterday; not that I cannot afford to give you the point-lace scarf, but because nearly all the Boujoulacs have been spendthrifts; five times they have married fortunes and run through with them. My father was an exception; he left me an ample estate, which has been much crippled by the war, it is true, but is still, as you know, enough even for my expensive tastes for occasional play. I have the passion under strong control. I set aside each year the sum which I can afford to lose, and I never go beyond it. It is my only extravagance. It seemed to me that we had outlived our family danger, and that I might allow myself this indulgence. But I have watched you closely of late, and I am convinced that the mania for unbridled expenditure will be for you a besetting and life-long temptation. Now, I want to make a fair bargain with you. I will give you a liberal allowance; if you will keep strictly within it, and will render an exact account of your expenses, I will give up cards."

A wave of great delight swept over Myrtle's face. We were quite alone in the coach, and she sprang from her seat and threw her arms about her father's neck. One would have thought that, instead of having been reproached for a weakness, she had achieved a triumph. Could it be that her wild extravagance was only assumed to effect this very end? I was not sure, but it looked like it.

"I accept the conditions," she cried, joyfully, "and Delight shall be witness to our agreement. You shall see how economical I can be. And, papa, if I think you are in danger, I will wear my Brussels scarf."

"And if that does not have the desired effect," replied the Colonel, "launch into extravagance again, and the fear that you may be yielding to our family curse will bring me to my senses."

So ended our visit to Brussels. We have returned to Antwerp, only to start to-morrow on an excursion to East and West Flanders as represented by the old towns of Bruges and Ghent.

CHAPTER III.

FLANDERS, GHENT, AND BRUGES.

WE found Mr. Blumenthal at our hotel on our return to Antwerp. He had made arrangements with his instructors for a little vacation, and offered to be our guide on our trip to Flanders. Of course we were very glad to accept his services, as he knows the language thoroughly, and has made the trip before. He brought his sketching materials with him, and has been making sketches for Myrtle all the way. Myrtle is in high spirits. I think she is greatly encouraged about her father. They love each other dearly, and I am sure the Colonel would do anything for the sake of his daughter.

Yesterday was a fête day at Antwerp, and in the evening there were fire-works on the Scheldt, a " nuit Venitienne " it was called. A pontoon bridge was laid across the river, and marine mines were exploded; all the shipping was decorated with flags and lanterns. Bengal lights were burned, which threw their bright reflections in long masses of brilliant wavy color upon the water, and gay boating parties rowed up and down. Mr. Blumenthal invited us to see the spectacle from a little steam yacht manned by some of the art students in historical costumes of the time of Charles V. The students had very good voices, and sang, as we glided along the magical river, student songs and bits from the popular operas. It was like fairyland. To-day the scene has changed, and in prosaic daylight we have been speeding over the peaceful country to this most matter-of-fact city of Ghent. And yet even here there is a certain atmosphere

DUTCH BOATS ON THE SCHELDT.

of quaintness and unreality. The medieval architecture carries us back into the old days. We can see the Hotel de Ville or City Hall from our window, and Myrtle has just taken up Motley to read his description of the city: —

HOTEL DE VILLE.

"Placed in the midst of cultivated fields, Ghent was surrounded by strong walls, — its churches and other public buildings were numerous and splendid. The sumptuous church of St. John or St. Bavon, where Charles V. had been baptized; the ancient castle whither Baldwin Bras de Fer had brought the daughter of Charles the Bald; the City Hall, with its graceful Moorish front; the well-known belfry, where for three centuries had perched the dragon, sent by the Emperor Baldwin of Flanders, from Constantinople, and where swung the famous Roland, whose iron tongue had called the citizens generation after generation to arms, — were all celebrated in the land. Especially the great bell was the object of the burghers' affection and generally of the sovereign's hatred."

The belfry is one of the most remarkable buildings in Ghent; it is a square tower surmounted by an octagonal campanile. We mounted to the summit and enjoyed a beautiful view of the city. We heard the chime of forty bells and saw the great one said to be Roland, though its refounding has erased the famous inscription, — "*Myn naem is Roeland; als ick klippe, dan is't brand; als ick luyde, ist victoire in Vlaenderland.*" — "My name is Roland; when I toll there is fire; when I ring there is victory in Flanders."

No wonder that Charles V. included Roland in his tyrannical punishment of the men of Ghent for their love of liberty. "How it brings it all back," said Myrtle, as we stood within the belfry; "just as it did to Longfellow. You remember how it seemed to him that

> "'—again the whiskered Spaniard all the land with terror smote;
> And again the wild alarum sounded from the tocsin's throat;
>
> Till the bell of Ghent responded o'er lagoon and dike of sand,
> I am Roland! I am Roland! there is victory in the land!'"

Mr. Blumenthal shook his head. "You have a lifely imagination," he said. "It is easy to say you see it all, but if you were to paint all that, you would have much trouble to make those costumes right; and then the composition, to bring in the figures in an artistic manner, the lesser subordinate to the important ones. I think I would rather be a painter of portraits."

"No doubt," Myrtle replied, "a single head is easier than a battle piece, but what is one a painter for if not to attempt grand subjects?

VAN ARTEVELDE AT HIS DOOR.

And the history of the Netherlands is full of them. There is the Battle of the Spurs of Gold, away back in 1302, when under the walls of Courtrai the Flemish routed the flower of the French chivalry. Think! seven hundred gilded spurs were picked up after the battle, proving that as many foreign knights had been slain. Then we come down to 1337, and James Van Artevelde, the doughty burgher who lived here in Ghent, and successfully defied the King of France. The Low Countries occupy such a little place upon the map, it would seem to have been so easy for France to have swallowed them up; and yet maintained such a sturdy independence all through their history, that we cannot help awarding their people a great respect."

Mr. Blumenthal looked at Myrtle admiringly. " How can it be? " he said; " you are a stranger to this country, and yet you are more acquainted to its history as I. You make me feel as if only great deeds were worth painting. I must think to what you have said."

Something in his look has made me think, — Myrtle does not suspect it, but, if I am not mistaken, this gentle art student is quietly losing his heart to her. It is a great pity, for Myrtle hates to be disagreeable to any one, but Mr. Blumenthal's broken English is sometimes so absurd, especially when he is very much in earnest, that I am sure that if he should propose to Myrtle she would laugh outright. Think of his saying, " Fräulein Boujoulac, you have inspired to me a feeling which I know not to express. Fräulein Boujoulac, I lay my heart to your foots; I beseech at you to pick him up." Dear me! it is too preposterous! but I see it coming.

BRUGES.

We left Ghent yesterday, visiting first, of course, the market-place and the cathedral, the château of the old counts, and Artevelde's statue. We remembered that the city was noted for its weaving, and went to see some rare old Dutch tapestries. A small piece which would have made a handsome portière was offered at a low price to Myrtle, and I expected to see her purchase it, but she said, "No, I must keep within my allowance," and then she exchanged such a look of loving trust with her father as was worth all the tapestries of Flanders.

When the Colonel asked us to choose a hotel from the guide-book, we spoke for the one in which Longfellow's Carillon was written.

> "Thus dreamed I as by night I lay
> In Bruges, at the Fleur-de-Blé."

MINE HOST OF THE
FLEUR-DE-BLÉ.

We were met by an unpoetic but jolly landlord, who made us comfortable in a homely, simple fashion; we heard the chimes in the night as Longfellow did. The city of bridges, as its name implies, is built along a number of canals. One of of these we followed into the country this morning, and picnicked near a picturesque windmill, which Mr. Blumenthal sketched for us. We bought some cream cheese and strawberries of a peasant, which eked out the luncheon we had brought from the city.

After luncheon the Colonel mounted to the top of the windmill for a view, and I took out one of Constant's stories of early times in the

VIEW IN BRUGES.

Netherlands, and, seating myself under a willow, was soon absorbed in the exciting tale. As I finished a chapter I happened to look up.

Mr. Blumenthal was seated opposite me on the bank of the canal, but he did not see me; his mane of light hair was tossed back and he was talking to Myrtle.

"I believe," he said, "that I have more talent than I have suspected; you have inspired to me a feeling which I know not to express." I started; these were exactly the words with which I had imagined he would begin his declaration; had it come? How embarrassing for me to overhear it. I coughed, but he went on. "I believe you could make of

A CONFIDENTIAL CHAT.

me a great painter. I have the dexterity, the technique. It is for your friendship to inspire me with the soul, the motive. Will you do this?"

"The impudence!" I thought to myself; "he asks her in the coolest way to devote her life to making him a genius. He is all wrapped up in self, and only cares for Myrtle because she can be useful to him." Something of this Myrtle must have felt, for, though her tone and manner were kindly, this was what she said, —

"I think, Mr. Blumenthal, that what you ask is hardly possible. Each of us is surely a complete being, with a mission of our own. Your inspiration will come, if you labor for it; and as for me, I must strive to find some means of expression for my own thoughts, some work that shall be all my own."

I felt that the situation must be now a little awkward for them both, and I came to their relief. This afternoon we are going to the picture gallery to see the Van Eycks and Memlings, and then good-bye to Bruges and the Fleur-de-Blé.

CHAPTER IV.

HOLLAND.

STEPPED GABLES OF ANTWERP.

A WEEK has passed since I made the last entry in my journal, and we are now at Rotterdam. We left Mr. Blumenthal at Bruges, to go back to the stepped gables of Antwerp, and continued our journey to Middelburg, on the island of Walcheren. It is a curious old town, with a highly ornamented town hall, an abbey, and many queer old houses. The wharves here, as in most of the Dutch ports, run up into the city. Indeed it is difficult to tell whether land or water predominates. Holland has fought a hand-to-hand battle

with the ocean for centuries. The land seems a mere fringe with
gulfs and bays extending into it from the ocean, and the Rhine, the
Scheldt, and the Meuse breaking through it on their way to the sea.
In many places the land is lower than the sea at high tide, and
defended at enormous expense and labor by dikes; these necessitate
constant repairs, and have from time to time been broken and the
country ravaged by tremendous inundations.   But the battle goes

WHARVES AT MIDDELBURG.

on, and the Hollanders are gaining on the water, for the rivers
bring down quantities of mud and sand, which they deposit at their
mouths; and the Hollanders, with the help of an army of windmills,
are pumping dry their lakes and swamps, walling in and filling up
bays, so that more land is made every year. We sailed along part of
the time through islands which we threaded by means of canals so
narrow that the steamer seemed to be passing over the ground.

HOUSE IN THE RENAISSANCE STYLE.

Sometimes we passed cities hiding behind their dikes, with only the steeples of the churches and the sails of the windmills peering at us above the embankments.

Rotterdam is a handsome city; its name comes from the river Rotte and the word dam, signifying dike, which forms the termination of the names of several Dutch towns. All Dutch towns have the reputation of being very clean, but Rotterdam had also a very new look; the houses on the Hoog Straat, or principal street, are large and modern looking, like those of Paris. It is probably the most enterprising city of Holland, and, next to Amsterdam, the richest. We are never tired of watching the shipping in the numerous canals, which also has a spick and span new appearance, every available bit of woodwork painted in gay colors, and the sailors perpetually scrubbing, and holy-stoning, and polishing. The coppers shine like gold, and the cabin windows have white muslin curtains. It is said that the Hollanders pay more attention to scrubbing their sidewalks than they do to personal cleanliness; but I think this a libel, for I have not yet seen a slatternly woman. The windows of the houses have a very attractive look, with their jardinières of bright geraniums.

Of course we have been at the picture gallery or museum, and have made so far a special study of Dutch landscapists. Myrtle suggested that we should begin in this way, by trying to become acquainted with the country, and after that with its people. As there is little variety in the land, the Dutch painters seem to have made much of the sky. We have, as a general thing, a quiet stretch of sand dune with low trees or windmills, and then a glorious cloud panorama. Ruysdael's pictures are quiet and restful; Cuyp's are more varied with cattle and shipping and glowing sunset effects. While we were trying to classify and understand the pictures, Myrtle happened to remark that she wished Mr. Blumenthal were with us, to help us understand them.

"Then you have quite forgiven him?" I asked, confessing what I had overheard at Ghent.

"That is not his fault," she replied, "but that of his education. Most Europeans seem to think that women were created simply to help men in accomplishing a career. The idea that they have souls and aspirations of their own to develop, never seems to have entered their heads."

A DUTCH LANDSCAPE.

"Myrtle," I asked, "do you think of studying art?"

"No, I have not the least bit of talent for it."

"Well, then, how do you intend to give expression to all the grand ideas with which your brain is teeming?"

"I shall have to go into partnership with some Vassar girl who is an artist or a writer, and agree to furnish her with subjects or plots, I presume."

"It seems to me this is just what Mr. Blumenthal wanted you to do for him."

"But he did not put it in that way. I was to be nothing, the cipher which was to give value to his life. If he had asked me in a fair American way, — let us work *together*, and I will do my best to express your thoughts, — why, that would have been a different thing altogether; but it was more like,—

> " ' Fishy, fishy, come bite my hook,
> I'll be captain if you'll be cook.'

ERASMUS.

He did not think of me at all in the friendship which he proposed, or even of what we could do together; he thought only of himself."

"Since the trouble is not in the plan itself," I remarked, "but only in the young man's way of presenting it, it is a pity that some one could not give lessons on polite and politic ways of putting things."

"Delight Holmes!" Myrtle exclaimed, "if you ever give that stupid young man any hints — but then, of course, you will have no opportunity to do so, and I shall probably never see him again, and it is just as well." But though she tripped into her own room humming a blithe tune, I have a fancy that she really does care, just a little.

We have been to see the statue of Erasmus, who was born in Rotterdam, and I have been trying to arrive at a correct estimate of his character. He was one of the greatest scholars of the 16th cen-

tury. He saw the abuses of the Romish church, but did not join the
Reformation. Motley says of him: "The Sage of Rotterdam was a
keen observer, but a moderate moralist. He loved ease, good company, the soft repose of princely palaces, better than a life of martyr-
dom and a death at the stake." He said of himself, "I am not of a
mind to venture my life for the truth's sake; all men have not
strength to endure the martyr's death. For myself, if it came to
the point, I should do no better than Simon Peter." While we cen-
sure him for knowing his duty and not doing it, let us beware lest we
judge ourselves.

His elegant Latin is world-renowned. The Colonel recited for
us some of his verses. It is said that Erasmus borrowed the horse
of an earnest Catholic, with whom he had had a discussion concern-
ing the transubstantiation of the bread by the saying of the mass into
the real body of Christ; and when his friend asked him to return it he
sent him these lines: —

> "Quod mihi dixisti
> De corpore Christi,
> Crede quod edas et edis,
> Sic tibi rescribo
> De tuo palfrido, —
> Crede quod habeas et habes."

"Can you turn that into English rhyme for me?" asked the
Colonel; and as a rather free translation I gave him, —

> What to me you have said
> Of Christ's body [in bread],
> You will eat if you only believe it,
> Thus to you I make answer
> Concerning your prancer, —
> Believe you receive, you receive it.

We had a little shock as we came away from looking at the
statue of Erasmus. We were in a cab, and another drove swiftly by

us. Its occupant had his head out of the window, and was hallooing something to his driver. We all recognized the hooky nose. It was Mr. Van Bergen. Fortunately he did not see us. "I thought he lived in Amsterdam," the Colonel said.

"I am glad he is here," Myrtle replied, "for I have quite dreaded going to Amsterdam, and now I shall not be expecting him to pop up there, like a Jack-in-the-box, at any instant."

"I can't see what has so prejudiced you against the fellow," the Colonel remarked; "he was an excellent poker player."

"Perhaps that is the reason for my dislike," Myrtle responded dryly.

THE HAGUE.

We have come to The Hague, only stopping on the way at Delft, to see the house where William of Orange was assassinated. It is a barrack now, and soldiers were lounging about the doorway; we felt a little timid about accosting them, but, although we could not speak Dutch, they seemed to know what we had come for, and showed us the staircase where the prince was shot, and the bullet marks on the wall, with the inscription. Then the guard dived into the interior and brought back a subaltern who spoke French and who answered all our questions very politely. He showed us the way to the church, and pointed out the tomb of William the Silent. It is a very grand affair, and contains the sculptured figure of the prince, with the little dog at his feet which saved his life by barking when Spaniards were about to assassinate him. There probably never was a man, — so the officer said, — so hounded by assassins, or one who played a grander part in history. From the time that he learned of the plot between Philip II. of Spain and Henry II. of France to crush Protestantism in their kingdoms, he took upon himself the defence of it in the Netherlands. Not because he was a Protestant at the time himself, but because he would not see defenceless people tortured and murdered for their religion. So, single-handed, he fought Philip II. and

the Inquisition, through splendid statesmanship and an intrepidity
that we wonder at and admire.   He must have considered the tremendous odds against him from the first, but, unlike Erasmus, he had
the spirit of a hero, and he died triumphant.

WILLIAM THE SILENT.

At The Hague, art is the chief interest.   We have seen more of
the Hollanders, of the peasants in their odd costumes and wooden
sabots, and here we have tried to study the life and the people
through the genre paintings.   There are quantities of small pictures
of interiors, finished so highly as to show infinite pains, and yet of
what we would consider trivial subjects.   Eating and drinking play

a great part, and kitchens with abundance of food ready for the cook, and shining copper and brass kettles. Green-groceries with mammoth cabbages and onions, are also favorite scenes, but the art of Holland is not all so material. I must quote what Thackeray says of this collection:—

"Here in the Hague Gallery is Paul Potter's pale eager face, and yonder is the magnificent work (the 'Young Bull') by which the young fellow achieved his fame. What hidden power lay in that weakly lad that enabled him to achieve such a wonderful victory? Potter was gone out of the world before he was thirty, but left this prodigy behind him. Napoleon carried off this picture to decorate his triumph of the Louvre."

If I were a conquering prince I would have this picture certainly, and the Raphael "Madonna" from Dresden, and the Titian "Assumption"

A BOY IN SABOTS.

from Venice, and that matchless Rembrandt of " The Dissection."

We stood before this last picture, unquestionably the greatest in the gallery. It represents a certain Dr. Tulp, to whom Rembrandt was much indebted, explaining to his pupils a lesson in anatomy. The first effect on looking at the painting is that of horror, for the light falls upon the corpse lying on the dissecting-table; the professor is pointing to the muscles with his forceps. Myrtle, after one shuddering glance, declared that she could not look at it, b came back again and again, fascinated not so much by the hor the thing on the table as by the wonderful painting of the fa the students following their master's grave explanations, with interest, professional enthusiasm, and respectful admiration of the learning of the doctor.

Rembrandt's other paintings interested Myrtle greatly, particularly his portraits of himself, and his religious pictures. We saw one of his etchings to-day, the "Ecce Homo," and were impressed by the character expressed in the different faces,—the hypocrite in the Pharisee, the rage in the mob, and the cowardice of Pilate, all contrasted

REMBRANDT.

by the simple nobility and resignation of Christ. "I remember now," said Myrtle, "how our art professor at Vassar, himself a Netherlander, loved this picture; but some way I had become impressed with the popular notion that Rembrandt was a painter of faces silhouetted against great masses of black, while, to my surprise, I find myself admiring the *tone* in his pictures even more than Rubens' glorious color."

I think Myrtle must be wrong in imagining that she has no talent througn·t; she seems to give the subject a great deal of earnest thought. of interi.vish we were to stay longer at The Hague. The place interests what wereatly. It seems more decidedly Dutch than Rotterdam, and

PROMENADE AT WEIMAR.

there are many queer customs which I have observed nowhere else. For instance, the people are very economical; they do not think of such extravagance as making a fire to cook breakfast. An old " water and fire woman " sits at the corner, and sells the maids a pot of boiling water and a burning piece of peat for a cent, with which she makes the coffee and boils the eggs, which, with rolls, and, possibly, cold meat, form the universal breakfast. I think we would loiter here longer but I have just received this letter from Miss Boylston, and so, after a trip to Scheveningen, a fishing village about two miles from The Hague, we shall hurry on to the Rhine.

Miss Boylston writes: —

MY DEAR MISS HOLMES, — Our friend Maud Van Vechten, now Mrs. Richard Atchison, writes me of your coming, and I am all impatience to meet a friend of Maud. We made our first trip through France and Spain together, and later we were in England together, to say nothing of the dear old Vassar days, which, in themselves, were enough to cement any friendship. And you and your friend are from Vassar too! I cannot express how eager I am to see and to talk over college news. I have been in Germany so long that I feel as if I had drifted back into some antediluvian period, and I must return to busy, bustling America ere long to prove to myself that I am really alive. And yet I love Germany, as I am sure you will. I have been studying in Weimar, with Herr Liszt, and it seems to me that I have never known what music was before. I do not know that you are particularly interested in music, but, if you are, you will find the soul of it all through this German land. At the larger cities the opera is almost always good, and very cheap. Good seats are fifty cents for plays, as a general thing, and sixty-two for operas, while, I believe, they can be obtained in the upper galleries as low as fifteen cents. Last winter we had "Faust," given complete in four nights ; a grand experience, and if you are fond of Wagner you have great things in store.

I am visiting here with a German lady, the Frau Generalin von Engel. Her husband, an officer of rank, was killed during the Franco-Prussian war. She is living a few miles from Coblentz, in a ritterhaus, something between a castle and a great farm-house. I made her acquaintance several years since, in Berlin, where I studied for a time in company with her daughter, and she insisted that I should spend a part of each summer with her here. I have told her of your coming, and she adds her most pressing invitation to mine that you will stop for a few days. I think you will enjoy such a visit, that it will give you a glimpse of German home life which you might not otherwise obtain, and I know it will give the good lady pleasure if you accept. She has several daughters at home, whom you will find interesting, cultivated girls, and a son who is given to farming. It is Frau von Engel's grief that her second and favorite son, who should, according to her military ideas, have entered the army, where he was sure of promotion, should have developed such a love for painting that he has given up all thought of a career, and has devoted himself to the study of art. This seemed to Frau von Engel so much like a selling of his birthright, and a lowering of the prestige of the family name, that the young man replied to her bitter reproaches that he would take for the present the humbler name of Blumenthal, to which he has also a right, until he had proved himself to possess sufficient talent to add lustre to the family title. The young man is studying at the Antwerp Academy.

I laid down the letter at this point with an exclamation of surprise. Shall I tell Myrtle what I have heard? That Mr. Blumenthal is so highly connected, and has so much spirit? On mature reflection, I shall do nothing of the sort. It would be just like Myrtle to decide not to go there, and I am sure it is not this dear lady's fault that she is Mr. Blumenthal's mother. How fortunate it is that he did not choose to claim the family name! Myrtle will never suspect that the Von Engels are in any way related to the little artist.

LATER.

The Boujoulacs have accepted Frau von Engel's invitation, and I feel like a conspirator. It will be fully a week before we reach there, for first we are to visit —

CHAPTER V.

SCHEVENINGEN. — AMSTERDAM AND COLOGNE. — MR. VAN BERGEN.

SCHEVENINGEN is a fishing village on the coast, which may be regarded as a suburb of The Hague. It is a great place for peasants in the strangest of caps and the showiest of ear-rings and other jewelry. They say we should see the place at Pinkster, a festival celebrated about the time of Easter; but as yet we have not been so fortunate as to see a kirmesse or peasant's fair. Scheveningen is, however, sufficiently interesting in its everyday life. Some of the peasant girls had very pretty faces ; the old women, as a rule, were preternaturally ugly. Scheveningen is divided into two parts; the old village, occupied by the fishing folk, and a modern water-

A SCHEVENINGEN BOY.

ing-place, frequented by the aristocracy. There could not be a stronger contrast between classes than that which we see here. We sat upon the beach and watched the strangers bathing, the children playing in the sand, the nurses watching them or gossiping, and as the tide was out I poked around in the little pools for new specimens of sea-weed. I found only coarse varieties, as I should have expected, from the cold waters of the North Sea. I am anxious to begin my botanical studies, or, at least, to know where I am to pursue them. Myrtle's brother writes that no ladies are received at

Bonn, but he hopes to induce one of the professors to act as my *Privat Docent,* or private tutor.

In old Scheveningen we were followed about unpleasantly by quite a mob of children. Wooden shoes, and cheeses round as cannon balls, seemed to be the chief articles of merchandise in the little shops, and the drying of herring the chief industry. It seemed to be a village of women and children, for the men were away with the

VIEW ON THE BEACH.

boats. We were glad to leave this settlement of Amazons, for they were loud-voiced and dirty, and, though their husbands had gone " sailing out into the west,

"Out into the west as the sun went down,"

the women, instead of watching them, seemed to prefer staring at us, and making uncomplimentary remarks, rather than wringing their hands and gazing after their spouses. The Flemish spoken here is

peculiarly unmusical. Here is a sentence which is usually a shibbo-
leth for all foreigners: —

"De schout van Scheveningen scheert de schapen acht en tach-
entig kleine kackeljes en de kat zij krabbelt de krullen van de trap-
pen af."

Amsterdam.

This city has been called the northern Venice, but it is a disor-
derly and unpicturesque
Venice, with none of the
calm and beauty of the
Queen of the Adriatic. It
is built on ninety islands,
and has a labyrinth of canals, and more bridges
than I can trust myself to
enumerate; but instead
of domes and campaniles,
it has only a vast army
of windmills beating their
arms like a host of pug-
nacious giants, challeng-
ing all the Don Quixotes

VIEW ON THE BEACH.

of the world to come and have it out with them in a boxing match.

The city is built on the shores of the Y, a gulf of the Zuyder
Zee, so called from its form. All Holland is low and flat enough,
but here the water predominates so much over the land that one
is tempted to accept Colonel Waring's derivation of Holland from
Hollowland. It is a very noisy city. Steam tugs are tooting
and whistling through the principal streets, people clamor and shriek
to make themselves heard above the rattling of drawbridges, the
clanging of chains, the roar of derricks, and the rumble of cordage.
Everywhere bales and bags, casks and boxes, were being laden and

unladen. Such racket and confusion must have been very distract-
ing to a philosopher, and yet Descartes wrote from here to his friend
Balzac, in 1629: —

"In this great city of Amsterdam, where I am now, and where
there is not a soul, except myself, that does not follow some commercial pursuit, everybody is so
attentive to his gains that I might live there all my
life without being noticed by anybody. I go walking
every day, amidst the con-
fusion of a great people,
with as much freedom and
quiet as you could do in
your forest alleys. Even
the noise of traffic does
not interrupt my reveries
any more than would that
of some rivulet."

The houses are tall and
rickety, the streets narrow

DUTCH WINDMILL.   and dark. The Ghetto, or

Jews' quarter, is the most filthly and sinister part of the city. Myrtle
and I clung tightly to the Colonel as we hurried through it.

The nondescript architecture of the steeples and towers of Amsterdam reminded us, as they did De Amicis, of Victor Hugo's comparison: "They build steeples by putting an inverted salad-bowl
upon a judge's cap, a sugar-bowl upon the salad-bowl, a bottle upon
the sugar-bowl, and an ostensorium (a golden stand from which the
Host is shown) upon the top of that."

DESCARTES AT AMSTERDAM.

We went to the diamond-cutting establishment to which Mr. Van Bergen had directed us, and found, as we had anticipated, that he was not there. We were told that he was to be travelling for the firm all summer throughout Germany, so it is possible that we may meet our *bête noir* any day, anywhere. We were shown the process of diamond-cutting; worthless looking pebbles flashed out before our eyes into glorious gems. A member of the firm told us that if we were anxious to meet Mr. Van Bergen, he might be found, or at least communicated with, at the shop of a Mr. Solomons, in Cologne, where money was advanced on precious stones; as it was our special desire not to see him, Myrtle was a little chagrined to see her father carefully take the address, ——strasse, near the Maria Farina cologne establishment. Myrtle has confided to me that she purposes we

SKETCHES IN HOLLAND.

shall make a very brief stop in Cologne, and she does not intend to give her father any chance to leave a card for Mr. Van Bergen. Myrtle is delighted that we are so near Germany, but I am sorry to leave queer old Holland, with its pretty peasant girls in their impossible costumes, the milk sellers with their dog-carts, the laundresses carrying their linen by the aid of a yoke fitted to their shoulders, the lace caps with lapels like rabbit's ears, and all the absurd but honest fashions of this quaint country.

COLOGNE.

Myrtle managed very adroitly, by first writing to Miss Boylston, and setting the date on which we might be expected at Coblentz. Then she insisted on stopping at Düsseldorf to see the gallery, though its chief treasures have been carried off to adorn the Pinacothek at Munich. In Düsseldorf we saw some delightful peasant pictures by Defregger, Vautier, and Knaus, three of the best painters of humble life in Germany. Ludwig Knaus' children in daisy-starred meadows are simply delicious. Vautier's are more serious in aim, and are full of character. This left us only three days, and, as the Colonel wished to spend at least two days with his son at Bonn, we could only give Cologne the time between the arrival of the morning and the departure of the afternoon train. Here again Myrtle manœuvred skilfully. We went first to see the grand, unfinished cathedral, which is ruinous in parts, while the towers are yet uncompleted. It was begun in 1248, and has been building with

GLIMPSE AT DÜSSELDORF.

intervals of neglect all these centuries. If finished, it is said it would have no equal in the world.

We found the slab which covers the remains of Marie de Medici, who died here in exile and poverty. The half light of the cathedral

CATHEDRAL AT COLOGNE.

interior was most impressive; the perfume of the incense, the twink-
ling tapers, the solemn notes of the organ, and the thought of the
dead queen, all combined to touch us profoundly. When we came
out into the garish daylight, Myrtle suggested that we should hunt up
St. Martin's Church, the favorite church of the people, with its quaint
towers and extinguisher cap. Then Myrtle found it absolutely necessary to make a pilgrimage to the church of St. Ursula, to see the
bones of the eleven thousand virgins, which modern research has
dwindled to eleven, owing to a misreading of the old Latin numerals.

After this, we lunched ; and then the Colonel felt the need of a
post-prandial nap, and sent Myrtle and me off for a drive about town
in a cab. Myrtle squeezed my hand with delight : "The crisis is
passed," she said. " Papa never has the enterprise to accomplish
anything in the afternoon ; we shall hear no more of Mr. Van Bergen
and his detestable pawn-shop."

(Marginal note. Poor Myrtle was over-confident; she little
imagined. at this time the suffering that this same little pawn-shop
would cause herself and father.)

Myrtle was in the gayest spirits as we drove about the city.
" The guide-book says that Cologne is the largest and wealthiest city
on the Rhine !" she exclaimed. " Think of it. Delight ! at last we
are really on the Rhine ; and the language is German, and not that
unpronounceable Flemish ! I am in love with the very signs. See,
Delicatessen, — doesn't that make your mouth water? *Musik
Papier* — perhaps Mendelssohn bought the paper on which he
wrote his scores at that very shop. *Leih Bibliothek,* — I can see the
books on the shelves, — Schiller and Goethe, Heine and Richter, and
Auerbach and Ebers. Even that announcement of Stuttgart sausage
and pretzels is so delightfully German that it loses all its vulgarity."

"It is rather a pity that the streets are so dirty," I said. " We
miss the street-sweepers of Antwerp."

"Yes," Myrtle replied ; " Cologne is noted for its unchristian smells.   This is probably the reason that drove the inhabitants to the manufacture of perfumes.   Who was it wrote ?

> " The river Rhine, it is well known,
>   Doth wash your city of Cologne.
>   But tell me, nymphs, what power divine
>   Shall henceforth wash the river Rhine ? "

So we finished our drive, and returned in high spirits to the hotel. As we passed the gentlemen's lounging-room, on our entrance, Myrtle clutched my arm ; and I was myself electrified to see the Colonel, whom we had imagined so safely disposed of, engaged in a quiet game of cards with a gentleman whose back was towards us, but whom we immediately recognized as Mr. Van Bergen.

ST. MARTIN'S CHURCH.

CHAPTER VI.

BONN, COBLENTZ, THE ENGEL RITTERGUT.

THE banks of the Rhine, from Cologne to Bonn, are flat and unin-
teresting. The Colonel declared that the river would not hold
a candle to the Mississippi; and as for real picturesqueness, it had
been terribly overrated, and was not to be compared to the French
Broad, in North Carolina, where he was "raised." But all his grum-
bling changed to quips and jokes when we reached the old university
town and were met by his son Joe, a really fine-looking young man.
Even Myrtle was roused from the depression into which that glimpse
at the hotel had plunged her. She is proud of her brother, as she
well may be, and we spent the day very pleasantly, viewing the old
town. He took us to the museum of Roman antiquities and to the
chemical laboratory, which is really very fine. Schlegel and Niebuhr
were professors here. The university has over one hundred professors, and upwards of seven hundred students. Prince Albert studied
here, and Joe says the Saxe Gotha Almanac is well represented
among the students. He was sorry not to introduce us to the sons
of several counts and hofmeisters and other illustriousnesses, but it is
vacation and they are away. Joe is an enthusiast over electricity, and
has been taking special work, preparing himself to be an electrical
engineer. "You are a plucky little thing to come over here to study
microscopy," he said to me. "Can you speak German?"

"After a fashion," I replied; "I have read 'Wilhelm Tell' and
'Egmont.'"

"With a dictionary," he interrupted, "and you think of each word

in English before you speak it. I've no doubt you are splendidly
prepared in botany; but unless you have a glib German tongue, I'm
afraid Professor Wissenschaft will not take to you. If it was Myrtle
here, I've no doubt she could make her way with half your knowledge; but you have such a frightened look, and are so tremendously
little."

"Thank you," I replied, "for reminding me of my insignificance."

"There, I'm always putting my foot in it; but I wish you were a
little more overpowering."

We called on Professor Wissenschaft, with the ill success which
Joe had predicted. He did not care
to take private pupils, and advised me
to apply to Professor Schwendeuer of
Berlin, who is the great authority on
fungi, algæ, etc. But first he was sure
it would be to my advantage to take
a special course in biology at Berne,
Zurich, or Geneva, the only places
really open to women, as to lectures
and degrees. I thanked him, accepted
his offer of a letter to Professor Schwen-
deuer, and came away a little discouraged, for Maud's friend, Dr. Victoria Delevan, wrote me that she would not advise any young girl
to study *alone* in Zurich; it is very unpleasant, on many accounts.
Joe tried to cheer me up, and thought that something might be done
at Heidelberg or Strasburg, where we are going.

PROFESSOR WISSENSCHAFT.

After supper, we strolled out, under the double avenue of chestnuts,
to the Schloss Poppelsdorf, and then turned into the beautiful Hof-
garten, full of grand old trees. Here we sat and chatted of different
parts of Germany, which I shall probably not see, unless I decide to
study in Berlin, for our present plan contemplates only the Rhine,
and possibly a corner of the Tyrol. Joe first studied German in

Hanover. The language of the north he thinks the best model for a foreigner, for it is clear-cut and exact, while the lisping character of the southern German accent, though, like our own southern dialect, very charming, he considers not so correct or so easily copied. The people of Hanover are very well affected toward the English, owing to their connection with them through the Hanoverian princes.

IN THE PUBLIC GARDENS AT BONN.

After a winter's residence here, Joe made a summer's tour through Germany, before settling down to his studies at Bonn. He touched off each of the principal cities with a few neat words of description. Potsdam, he said, was identified with the memory of Friedrich der Grosze; Berlin, with the present court, the Green Vaults, and the famous promenade, Unter den Linden; Dresden, with its art gallery, famous above all for the Madonna San Sisto, and Correggio's Magdalen; with the porcelain works at Meissen, and with its fine photographs; Leipsic, with its university, its musical conservatory, and its printing; Nuremberg, with metal work and carving; Munich, with modern artists, especially Kaulbach and Piloty, and with its fine art galleries. There are twenty-one university towns. At Essen, on the Ruhr, are the great foundries where the Krupp guns are made.

He says when we are at Heidelberg we must run across to Stuttgart, and suggested that we should now make an excursion up the Moselle. "I rowed up as far as Treves with my friend Blumenthal last summer," he said. I wrung my hands under my shawl, fancying that now the secret that Mr. Blumenthal was the son of Frau Von Engel would certainly be divulged. But Myrtle, not caring to hear more of Mr. Blumenthal, rose and walked away down a little path for a view of the Rhine; and I had an opportunity to explain my small plot. It happened that, although we had told Joe of our invitation to visit Frau Von Engel, her relationship to Mr. Blumenthal had not been explained, probably because Joe supposed that his sister already understood it. As I told him the whole story, how his friend had offended Myrtle and my conviction that she could never have been persuaded knowingly to visit at his home, he laughed merrily. "You girls are all alike," he said, "always full of mysterious plots. I admire your strategy, for Blumenthal is a good fellow after all, and Myrtle is sure to like his mother. There is a picture of his which he has lately sent on sale at the art store in Bonn. The dealer knew him in student days. I wish father would buy it."

The next day, Joe took us to see the picture. It was called "News from the Front," and was a scene from Mr. Blumenthal's childhood. When his father, a Prussian officer, followed Moltke to France, he took with him a cage of pigeons; after each German victory, he liberated one, which flew straight to the home dove-cote, carrying under its wing a little packet containing the latest news. One day a pigeon came, with no letter, but with a shred of some black stuff about its neck, and a lock of the officer's hair under its wing. Then the poor lady knew that her husband was dead, and that his faithful servant, who could neither read nor write, had sent her this message.

The picture represented the arrival of the pigeon. The widow was leaning from an ivy-framed window tempting the bird to approach, while her agonized gaze was fastened upon the fluttering

GODESBURG.

black signal. At the lady's side was the wondering face of a boy, which suggested that of the young artist.

Myrtle was struck by the painting. "He has more imagination than I thought," she said. "I would like to buy the picture."

The Colonel demurred. "Can you do it and keep within your allowance?" he asked. Myrtle flushed, and looked at her father strangely for a moment.   I thought she was going to say, "Have you kept your part of the agreement?" but she restrained herself; and the Colonel left the store, apparently unconscious of anything unusual in his daughter's demeanor.   Joe has decided to make the trip up the Rhine with us, and will join us at the Engel Rittergut.

We came on to Coblentz yesterday.   It is an important town, situated at the junction of the Moselle with the Rhine.   We begin now to approach the romantic regions, and to see ruins and castles.   At Godesburg, near Bonn, we saw a high dungeon tower, standing alone amid the crumbling arches which once formed a part of the edifice. This tower is at least ninety feet high, and, we were told, commanded a fine view of Drachenfels in the Siebengebirge.   We passed Königs-winter, and Nonnenwerth, and Rolandsdeck, the scene of Campbell's poem.   The legend runs that Hildegund hearing of Roland's death in Spain, took the veil at Nonnenwerth; the rumor proving to be false just too late.   Roland, returning, built himself a hermitage, where he could look down upon the island, and hear the choral service of the nuns.   William Black has written a little poem on Nonnenwerth, beginning, --

> "Knight Roland sate above the Rhine ;
> O bride of God that walkest there,
> Gone is the gold-light of thy hair ;
> And never more thy blue eye's shine
> May rise to meet the love of mine."

We stopped for a few hours at Andernach, the delight of all artists.   We saw several of them.   One, seated in the old Convent kitchen, splashing in the rich browns of the interior in water-color; another, making a fine pen-and-ink sketch of the town; and a third, in the village street, was painting in oils the portrait of a wrinkled crone, while a tribe of the prettiest and plumpest of children, for whom Andernach is especially noted, were critically examining his work.

IN ANDERNACH.

We were met at Coblentz by Otto Von Engel, Mr. Blumenthal's older brother. He is a tall, well built man, who speaks French fluently. He had come for us with an open carriage; and he took us to drive across the long lava bridge which spans the Moselle, and up to the fortress of Ehrenbreitstein, a citadel, which fully exemplifies Germany's

EHRENBREITSTEIN.

military strength. "My father was stationed here," Mr. Von Engel explained, "and it was to have his family near him that he purchased from the government the rittergut where we now live."

A rittergut, as he explained it, is a sort of farm, with a manor house, to possess which, in itself, is a sort of patent of nobility; and a Gutbesitzer is a gentleman farmer. "When the Franco-Prussian war broke out, my father was ordered to the front," he continued, "and was killed in the attack on Bougival, in the very last fighting, before the taking of Paris."

Myrtle murmured something sympathetic, and added, "It seems that all the German acquaintances we have made so far, have lost their fathers in the late war."

"We are a military nation," Mr. Von Engel replied. "What else can we expect? But Bismarck has done good; he has accomplished his great plan, the unification of Germany, and that —"

"Makes it easier for the children who study geography," Myrtle interpolated mischievously. "It must have been very hard for you, when a boy, to remember all the kingdoms, and grand duchies, and principalities. That is what consoles papa for the failure of the Southern Confederacy. The United States once dissolved, we would have separated into ever so many different countries; and think how hard it would have made the 'bounding' for the school children of the next generation."

THE GNÄDIGE FRAU VON ENGEL.

"There is a higher thought hidden in your pleasantry," the young man said, gravely. "The fewer countries, the fewer wars. We shall reach the time, by and by, when there will be only one nation, the entire human family." "And this nation of the future will be German?" Myrtle asked. "Assuredly"; and at this he drew rein before a picturesque country house, through whose park we had been driving. On the steps stood an elderly lady, the Gnädige Frau Von Engel, very plainly dressed in a short black silk gown, her white hair combed back under a black silk cap, with a ruche of the same material. She wore large unbecoming spectacles; but a kindly smile lurked in the wrinkles of her very positive mouth, and she welcomed us most kindly. Miss Boylston came forward and presented Professor Hammer, an old musician, and the daughter of the house, the Countess Stoltzenberg, a tall elegant appearing young woman, dressed, in contrast to her mother, in the height of the Berlin fashions. It has struck me since I have been here, that German people, if this family can be taken as an example, do not pay great attention to dress. The fashionable allow themselves to be clothed by their dressmakers, without considering whether the mode is especially becoming; and such good dames as the Frau Von Engel go on dressing as they did in their youth, simply from convenience. The result is not so artistic as the dressing in America, but it saves a deal of mental worry; and they are so delightfully unconscious of their personal appearance, and devote themselves so thoroughly to having a good time, as if clothing were a matter of natural growth, like plumage.

PROFESSOR HAMMER.

I shall write of Miss Boylston later; at present, I can only say that she looks very clever, and I am a trifle afraid of her. She played for us last evening Liszt's Rhapsodie Hongroise No. 2, one of her favorite selections, I am sure, for her very heart seemed to go into her fingers.

Professor Hammer watched her with the keenest interest; the Countess and Miss Boylston have been his pupils, and it is easy to see which he prefers. He confided to me that she has a wonderful talent, "but," he added, "a great catastrophe menaces her, — a marriage. Bah! such a woman has no right to marry."

I wonder whom Miss Boylston is to marry; perhaps Otto Von Engel. Frau Von Engel is to give a Kaffeeklatsch this afternoon to some of her neighbors, and we will see a little of German society. So far, I find everything German intensely interesting. The cham-

ber which has been assigned to Myrtle and to me, in which I am
now writing, is as quaint and queer as one could well imagine.   One
side is occupied by two single beds standing foot to foot, each with a

THE COUNTESS.

puffy eider-down quilt like a pin-cush-
ion; the pillows studiously covered by
the chintz spreads.   The room is pa-
pered with a vine pattern, green and
white, very fresh and bowery; there
are white muslin curtains at the windows, which look out upon the dove-
cote, and are continually crossed by
the shadows of flitting wings.   Nearly
in the centre of the room, is a monumental arrangement in white porcelain,
which Myrtle thought was a pedestal
for a statue. but which we soon ascertained was a German stove.   There was
no fire in it, and a jug containing a
bouquet of roses stood on the snowy
slab.   The *Dienstmädchen* (servant)
has just appeared with a cup of chocolate; as though we could
eat anything more after the very abundant *abendbrod* (supper).
It shows their kindliness of heart all the same.   Frau Von Engel had
much to say of Joe Boujoulac, and quite won the Colonel's heart by
her admiration for his *liebenswürdig* (son).   We have fallen into
kindly hands, and I foresee a delightful visit.

CHAPTER VII.

A KAFFEEKLATSCH, AND A MYSTERIOUS OCCURRENCE.

SOMETHING very extraordinary has happened; but I must relate all in regular order.

The Kaffeeklatsch was very interesting. It was a sort of four o'clock tea. Only ladies were present, most of them wives of officers, for Frau Von Engel's acquaintance is chiefly military. Some of the gentlemen drove up to the door with them, and then incontinently departed. They would have faced the French chassepots sooner

A GERMAN OFFICER. than our society, and yet they were handsome, burly men, with fierce moustaches, and their coat fronts presented a startling array of decorations; stars, crosses, and ribbons of every color. I am becoming accustomed to hearing German, so that I can now gather ideas from the waves of sound, which formerly broke around me as unintelligibly as the breakers on a rocky coast. The conversation turned on the last war. "You should have seen Coblentz then," said an old lady, the Frau Baronin Von — something or other; "it was a depot of supplies, and forwarding station. The town was filled with troops, going, coming, constantly moving; but always full. It would have done your heart good to see the provisions which the burgomasters of the different districts sent in. Long trains of forage, and wagons of beer, and hams, and sausage, and cheese, and wine, and poultry, and bread. *Lieber himmel!* how often I have said, 'Of course our soldiers will fight if they are fed like that.'"

Another, prettier and more romantic woman chimed in, "Ah! yes; the soldiers had all they could eat, but it was sad all the same. They were such handsome fellows, and their-wives and their sweethearts often came as far as Coblentz to bid them good-bye. I was only a *Backfischen* (schoolgirl) then, but I was much impressed by the farewells. Every third person you met was crying or kissing good-

BISMARCK.

bye, or hiding a souvenir in his breast. I was eight years old, and I determined on the spot that I would some day marry a *wohlgeborn Hauptmann* at least."

"'J'aime les militaires,'" hummed Frau Von Engel; "how any man can adopt any other profession, is beyond my poor comprehension."

"And how heavenly is the uniform!" exclaimed another enthusiastic lady; "the helmet, which may serve as a drinking-cup. But for something *wunderschön*, quite ravishing, give me a regiment of Hussars; with their superb horses richly trapped, and the splendor of their dress, equal to that of the Knights of the Middle Ages. You have heard of the Hussar who, visiting his fiancée, carelessly placed his helmet too near the fire, and the fine horse-hair plume was burned

THE KAFFEEKLATSCH.

off, and how the girl cut off her own beautiful black hair to supply its place? Well the story is quite true; I knew the lady. Fortunately, her hair grew out again thicker and more lovely than before."

"*Ach! liebes kind*, the Hussars are very well," said one lady, "but what can be finer than the uniform of the Bavarian Jaegers; blue hunting suits with green plumes, and how they spoiled their uniforms at the battle of Woerth, poor fellows. They were under the command of General Steinmetz."

"They were all brave fellows," said the daughter of our hostess, the Gnädige Gräfin; "my father was in the famous Guard Corps, commanded by Prince Friedrich Karl. I can remember now how they sang the *Wacht am Rhein*, the night before they left Coblentz."

All this time, trays of cakes and sweetmeats were being constantly passed by Katchen, the countess's maid, who wore a wonderful cap over her yellow braids. The chattering did not in the least interfere with the eating. A Frau Burgermeisterin absorbed, according to my strict count, five cups of coffee, ten different kinds of cake, three dishes of ice-cream, several glasses of wine, besides an unlimited quantity of candies. Frau Von Engel constantly pressed her with "*Bitte, bitte,* you eat *gar nichts,*" and she excused her lack of appetite quite gravely, explaining that she had just come from a lunch party, and was on her way to a grand dinner at the house of a Frau Directorin. How the Germans do enjoy eating! Frau Von Engel told me, with a pathetic little sigh, that she sent her husband a box of goose sausages and pickled sauer-kraut, of which he was very fond, and she could almost have forgiven the French if they had only given him time to eat them before he was killed!

We have four regular meals per day, and I can well believe the story that the commander-in-chief of the Prussian army, when he billeted his officers and men on ruined Strasburg, demanded that each person should have two breakfasts, — the first, of coffee and rolls, the second, of soup and a solid dish of meat with vegetables; a dinner of soup, two kinds of meat, vegetables, dessert and coffee, with two bottles of good wine, and five cigars. This contributed more than anything else to fan the hatred of the French for the troops invading Alsace.

I was quite thankful when the party was over, and glad to escape with Myrtle into the open air, for Otto Von Engel wished to show us his gardens. Myrtle took out her camera, which has been neglected of late, and took some photographs of the buildings, and of the head gardener, Heinrich, who was dressed in his holiday suit, as he had been serving as gate-opener for the company.

Otto is proudest of his tulips, and was surprised that the mania for this flower had subsided in Holland. He gave Myrtle a bulb, which, he said, at one time would have brought a fabulous price, as the flower is quite black, and, though common now, was formerly very rare. Myrtle asked to have it potted, as she was impatient to see the blossom. Otto placed it in earth for her, and cautioned her not to be so impatient as to pull it up every day to see whether it were growing.

Myrtle, to my mind, was the most beautiful girl at the Kaffeeklatsch, and she was unquestionably the best dressed. She wore her diamond cross, and although the Colonel expressed himself again as dissatisfied with the setting, and wished Myrtle would not be so obdurate about having it remounted,

HEINRICH.

none of the noble ladies wore more magnificent gems.

And now comes the mysterious occurrence. Myrtle thinks she left the cross rather carelessly on the dressing-table at night, and when we awoke in the morning it was not to be found!

· I either dreamed it, or I sleepily saw some one standing by the toilet table during the night, but my impressions were so confused that they were worthless.

Myrtle was greatly troubled; but she would not allow me to mention it to Frau Von Engel or to her father. "I do not want to throw suspicion unjustly upon the servants, or to alarm papa

causelessly," she said; "perhaps I mislaid it, and I want to take a thorough hunt through my belongings before I raise the alarm."

The windows of our room open upon a little balcony, which runs along past the Colonel's room to the corner of the building. Myrtle had placed her tulip on this balcony, and I noticed that it had been over-

THE RITTERGUT.

turned and the bulb carelessly replaced. "Whoever took your cross entered by the balcony," I said, pointing to the flower-pot. Myrtle turned deadly pale, but said nothing. It seemed to me that I read her thoughts, and that a suspicion that her father had taken the cross, possibly to pay a gambling debt, flashed at that instant across her mind.

At the breakfast table, Frau Von Engel proposed that we should

THE PORTA NIGRA.

make an excursion of three or four days by steamer; up the Moselle to Treves, where there are some Roman ruins, stopping also at other interesting places *en route*.

The Colonel professed himself very sorry, but said that he had promised his son to return to Bonn and spend a few days with him. (I was morally certain that this was only an excuse to carry the cross to Cologne.) His engagement, he protested, need not in any way interfere with our enjoying the trip. He was very gay and chatty, professed himself delighted with Germany, and said he would like nothing better than to have a position in the German army. This delighted Frau Von Engel, who was sure that it could be managed.

"Have you any messages for your brother?" the Colonel asked of Myrtle, shortly before he left. Myrtle drew her father aside from the others. "I want you to purchase that picture of Mr. Blumenthal's for me," she said, speaking rapidly and in a constrained way. "You noticed that I wore my Brussels lace scarf at the Kaffeeklatsch. The Countess admired it greatly; she is a connoisseur in lace, and asked me where she could obtain a scarf like mine. I told her that I was tired of it, and it was at her service. She insisted on my accepting the sum which I paid for it, and this makes it possible for me to purchase the picture without going beyond my allowance."

"Very well, my dear," said the Colonel; "I shall be rather glad to have the scarf out of the way, especially as you were never to wear it without conveying to me a disagreeable reproach."

Myrtle looked her father steadily in the face, and said, with only a slight tremble in her voice, "I ought to tell you that I have lost my diamond cross."

"What!" he exclaimed, starting violently. "Have you informed Frau Von Engel? A reward ought at once to be offered for its recovery."

Myrtle's glance fell. "I thought if I waited it might be returned, or perhaps I may find it," she hesitated.

The Colonel gave his daughter a swift, suspicious glance.   "You are possibly right," he said, in a constrained voice.   "We will wait before making an outcry."

It was a strange tableau to take place between father and daughter, and I was grieved to have witnessed it.   I was not sorry that the interview was interrupted by the arrival of a visitor, and by joyful outcries from the Von Engels.   Turning, we were surprised to see Joe paying his respects to the Countess, and receiving the welcomes of the family.

Frau Von Engel clapped her hands joyfully.   "This is just as it should be," she cried; "now your father has no excuse to absent himself from us, and you are just in time to join our excursion. *Nicht wahr ?* "

"With all my heart," Joe replied.   " In what direction is the excursion?   I have thrown over my vacation cramming, and obtained leave of absence for a month.   Ah! my *bemooste haupt!* " he cried, catching sight of Otto and embracing him affectionately.

"Moss-covered head! what does he mean by such an expression?" I asked of Miss Boylston.

"It is a college term of respect given to the oldest student.   I used to hear it frequently in Weimar," she replied, "but, since Otto has devoted himself to agriculture and gardening, it is intended as a little play upon words; an insinuation that he has vegetation on the brain, I presume."

It was quite true that the Colonel had now no excuse to absent himself from us.   There was nothing for him to do but to pretend to be perfectly satisfied.   He flew about with a rather overstrained gayety; and I thought, with a certain grim satisfaction, that the diamond cross was probably safely buttoned inside his waistcoat, and would have no chance of finding its way to Mr. Van Bergen, until our return from Treves.

CHAPTER VIII.

THE MOSELLE. — AN EXPLANATION.

WE formed a rather imposing procession, as we embarked on the little steamer which is to take us up the Moselle. As the servants stowed the lunch hampers on board, I noticed that there was one for every member of the party. Frau Von Engel says the inns are execrable, but it does not seem possible that we can consume such a store of provisions. Our first stop was at Carden, where we took carriages for the famous Castle Elz, one of the oldest and grandest in Germany. The entire river had been one lovely winding panorama of terraces, covered with vines and verdant intervals.

MISS BOYLSTON.

As our party was a large one, it broke up, naturally, into groups. I noticed, with satisfaction, that Frau Von Engel and Myrtle seemed to take to one another; there is something about the elder lady's quaint frankness, her heartiness and honesty, which fascinates Myrtle, while I can see that the Frau admires Myrtle's gentleness and deference. She looked lovelier than ever too in her shade hat, with a new pensiveness, which is not natural, but has lately come into her eyes. Poor Myrtle! while she is talking to the Frau, she is thinking of her father, who is devoting himself politely to the Countess; and her eyes follow him with a loving trouble, which I alone understand. The four took the lead in an open carriage, while Miss Boylston, Professor Hammer, Joe, and I, took a second, Otto climbing to the driver's seat. We followed a ravine for about a mile, when the peaked turrets of the castle came in view. It is one of the most satisfactory realizations of what a feudal castle should be; is very tall and imposing, and is built upon an island, the little stream flowing around it and washing its foundations. It is the home of one of the noblest German families, with whom the Von Engels are slightly acquainted, and from whom they have permission to visit the castle at any time, a privilege not always accorded to the ordinary traveller.

WITH A NEW PENSIVENESS.

The interior of the castle is a maze of winding passages, galleries, and apartments. We strayed about from room to room, and out upon the roof. Joe saw his sister looking sadly from a turret window, her thoughts evidently withdrawn from the lovely landscape, and he sang lightly,—

> "Ich weiss nicht was soll es bedeuten
> Dasz ich so traurig bin."

Myrtle crimsoned and turned away.

"What is the matter with Myrtle?" he asked of me. "She seems uncommon grumpy. Doesn't she like the Von Engels?"

For a moment I thought of confiding in him. Would it not be

easy for him to discover the whereabouts of the lost cross, or at least so watch and guard his father that he would be unable to dispose of it, or to indulge in the dangerous society of Mr. Van Bergen. The next instant I felt that this would be a disloyalty to Myrtle, that the poor girl would prefer to walk the thorny way alone, and I turned aside the inquiry.

As we left the castle, Miss Boylston was thrown with Joe, quite accidentally as it seemed to me, and I was left with Professor Hammer, who was very much out of sorts, and not at all amusing. When Miss Boylston joined us, as she did for the carriage drive, he brightened up, and we chatted of music and musicians.

I was anxious to hear about her stay at Weimar, and of Liszt. She showed me his autograph in a little pocket-album: —

"Mit den besten glückwünschen zu ihren beständigen kunstlerischen erfolgen." (With best wishes for your artistic career.) Professor Hammer growled under his breath, glaring at Joe: "Nothing in the way of it, — nothing at all, — but that monkey."

Miss Boylston says that Herr Liszt is the kindest-hearted man in the world. Some one writes that he found him standing on one of the street corners in Paris, holding the broom of a crossing sweeper. On being asked what he was doing, he replied, "I had no change less than a five-franc piece; the little man has gone to get it changed, and in the meantime I am taking care of his broom."

Wagner is Liszt's son-in-law. Miss Boylston admires Wagner's music exceedingly. I did not dare tell her that to me it is a barbaric blare of sound.

I was startled by Wagner's creed, which Professor Hammer gave us: "Ich glaube an Gott, Mozart, und Beethoven."

The conversation turned upon Mendelssohn.

"You know," said Miss Boylston, "that in his youth he was musical director at Düsseldorf, and at Cologne. It was there that some of his first successes were achieved. His father's letters from Düs-

seldorf describing the Musical Festival of 1833," Miss Boylston added,
"are delightful in their expression of the first delight and surprise over
his son's triumphs.   The entire neighboring country swarmed into
Düsseldorf to attend the festival.   A large hall was built in a beer-
garden outside the city, and here, between the first and second parts
of 'Israel,' the audience 'rush into the garden,' and, after the German
fashion, consume vast quantities of *Maitrank*, seltzer-water, curds and
whey, etc.   Then a loud flourish is blown from the orchestra, and
again Israel cries to the Lord.   But the Germans are as sincere in
their love of music as their fondness for eating.   The young *General
Musikdirektor* won his first laurels, literally, in this beer-garden.
His friends from the chorus held him while a laurel wreath was
placed on his head; the orchestra especially were wild with enthusiasm, the Cologne people carried him away to their city to do him
honor, and the tide of popular applause swept him from obscurity to
the place he now occupies throughout Germany and the world."

We spent the night at Trarbach, about half way between Coblentz
and Treves, and in the early morning climbed to the ruins of the
Graefinburg, that overlook the town.   Joe was again Miss Boylston's
escort.   "They are always together, those two," grumbled Professor
Hammer, as we toiled along in company.   When we reached the
summit, we threw ourselves on the grass and enjoyed the view of the
river.   Unfortunately, the wind brought our friends' conversation
toward us, though they sat at a little distance.   They were comparing this ruin to Drachenfels.   "I never see that castled crag," said Joe,
" without thinking of Byron's lines:—

> " ' Above the frequent feudal towers,
> Through green leaves, lift their walls of gray ;
> And many a rock which steeply towers,
> And noble arch in proud decay,
> Look o'er this vale of vintage bowers ;
> But one thing want these banks of Rhine,
> Thy gentle hand to clasp in mine.' "

TRARBACH.

"*Donnerwetter!*" exclaimed the Professor; so energetically that Miss Boylston looked up and asked, "Do you think we are going to have a storm?"

I could not resist a laugh. "It was the poetry," I explained; "I do not think the Professor is fond of Byron."

So it is Joe, and not Otto, of whom the Professor disapproves. I don't know exactly why, but I do not quite like it. Miss Boylston is good and talented, but I suspect she is older than Joe; and then she is so calm and self-contained, and he is such a jolly fellow. Still, I do not see that their affairs at all concern me, or the Professor either.

Myrtle has been taking photographs to-day, as we have passed a number of picturesque towns and ruins. One of the most composed looking views, as though it were arranged for theatrical effect, was the village of Berncastel, with its towers upon the hill.

JOE.

All of these ruins have their legends. That of the Castle of Graefinburg, which we saw this morning, is that it was built with an archbishop's ransom. The archbishops of Treves were a tyrannical, high-handed set of men, who lorded it over all the Moselle valley. They subdued the proud lords of Elz so that they were mere retainers; but the Countess Loretta of Sponheim resisted the episcopal sway, and once when the Archbishop of Treves was being rowed down the river, she caused the barge to be stopped by a chain stretched under the water, and, in the confusion of the moment, her men rowed out and took the prelate prisoner. He was treated reverently, but obliged to pay a heavy ransom.

We have now reached this pre-historic old city. We go back far enough when we know that it was the capital of the Treviri, one of the tribes of Gauls which Cæsar conquered. The Roman ruins are in a remarkably good state of preservation; the finest among them is the "Porta Nigra." The Professor, and Otto, and Joe, were soon deep in controversy over it; but the Colonel said he cared more for

CONFIDENCES.

forts and battle-fields, and manifested very little interest in the fine Basilica, the Baths, and the Amphitheatre.

I think we really enjoyed the cathedral, with its fine shady cloisters, more than these classic remains. We found the "Evil-doer's chair," a particularly uncomfortable stone seat, in which malefactors, who sought the sanctuary as a place of refuge, were obliged to sit; and we were shown a sacred relic, the seamless coat of camel's hair

BERNCASTEL.

said to have been worn by our Saviour. We spent two days at Treves, and would have enjoyed a week.

Frau Von Engel and Myrtle are more inseparable than ever. I saw them together in the Amphitheatre yesterday, apparently indulging in earnest confidences. I suspect that the secret is out, and that they have been talking of Mr. Blumenthal.

LATER.

I was writing up my journal in the cloisters, and had just penned the above sentence when Myrtle entered. "I have been looking for you everywhere," she said. "I have just discovered a most remarkable coincidence. Max Blumenthal is Frau Von Engel's son!"

"Indeed," I replied, as innocently as I could; "how very surprising!"

"Is it not? It only shows that the unexpected is what is sure to happen. This is how it came about. Frau Von Engel was telling me what a good son Otto is, but, in spite of this, that she loved almost better her second son, who had disgraced her. 'How disgraced you?' I asked. 'He has persisted in adopting the occupation of an artist, instead of the career of a soldier.' And then I grew quite warm, and told her how much nobler I considered the artist's profession. 'He brings nature and God's work close to us, if he is a landscapist,' I said; 'he makes noble deeds immortal, if he is a historical painter; he gives us our loved ones to stay with us, even after they have passed to heaven, if he is a portrait painter.' 'But if he is only a realist?' she asked; 'if he paints faces just as he finds them, without composition, and without imagination?'

"I do not remember exactly what I replied. I know I astonished myself by defending realism. 'How better can he depict character,' I asked, 'the consequences of certain courses of living and thought, than to copy faces from life, faces scarred by evil deeds, or transfigured by noble thoughts? It seems to me he becomes a great teacher;

showing us the heaven or hell in each human face, warning, or setting examples in every picture.'

"I think Frau Von Engel was very glad to be convinced that she
has been longing after this favorite son, and regretting her own pride
and hardness of heart, for she kissed me quite rapturously, and said
that she would write to him at once that she had changed her views.
All this time I had no suspicion of whom she was speaking, but after
this I chanced to mention the picture at Bonn, 'News from the
Front,' and I described the face of the lady watching the circling
pigeon, — the sudden dismay and grief with which it was filled. As I
spoke, the same expression came into Frau Von Engel's. '*Lieber
Himmel!* It must be that my son painted it. It was thus that I
received the news of my widowhood.' Then I had all I could do
to fan her, for she seemed quite faint. Fortunately, Otto came up
just then with the lunch-basket, and she refreshed herself with some
strong coffee. After that, she explained quite volubly how Max had
renounced the family name temporarily. 'But he shall take it again,'
she cried; 'this picture has gained it for him. I will send for it and
for him at once. *Liebe fräulein*, you will stay and see our family
rejoicings.' It was with difficulty that I could explain to her the
impossibility of this, and indeed we must start again on our Rhine
journey as soon as we return to Coblentz, for I would not meet Mr.
Blumenthal just now for a great deal."

So this is the end of the little romance which I had planned.
One good end, at least, has been accomplished, in the reconciliation of
mother and son. Myrtle has resigned her purpose of purchasing the
picture, in favor of Frau Von Engel. We all return to Coblentz to-
morrow, as we shall not stop *en route*. The descent of the river can
be made in about twelve hours. Myrtle is all impatience to be off,
for Frau Von Engel, instead of writing, has sent her son a telegram
demanding his instant presence.

CLOISTER OF CATHEDRAL OF TREVES.

CHAPTER IX.

THE RHINE, FROM COBLENTZ TO RÜDESHEIM. — AN UNEXPECTED
MEETING.

WE are strangers in a strange land once more, for with the friendly Von Engels we seemed almost at home. We left the rittergut yesterday, and are now steaming up the beautiful Rhine, our party increased by the addition of Miss Boylston and Joe.

When we parted, the Countess expressed her intention of soon returning to her own home in Munich, and gave us all a very urgent invitation to visit her there. She described her husband and her children. She only waits to see her brother, and will take Professor Hammer back with her, as her husband has just written that he has obtained a position of kapellmeister for him. It would be a rare chance to see something of city life and of high society, but we are not likely to profit by it. Joe is strongly in hopes that I will find an opportunity for study at Heidelberg, and if I do I must settle down to it at once.

Joe is a very useful adjunct for the carrying of the camera, shawl-straps, etc., but he draws a line at Myrtle's tulip, and declares, not without reason, that loading one's self with potted plants upon a journey is a little too absurd. Myrtle tucked it away in the lunch-basket, hoping that he would not discover it, but he has threatened that if she ever tricks him into carrying it again he will throw it into the river. I think Joe is a little cross because Myrtle hurried us away so suddenly from the rittergut; he wanted to meet his friend, and declared that it looked as if we were running away from him, when he is expected so soon. "I would not hurt Blumenthal's feelings for the world," he said; "he is such a good-hearted fellow. He gave a lecture at the deaf and dumb asylum the day before he left for Antwerp." Myrtle laughed sarcastically. "A lecture to the deaf and dumb!" she repeated.

"Yes, my dear, a lecture, made up of pictures. He drew them as rapidly as you could talk, and told all sorts of amusing stories by one scene following another. His audience laughed from beginning to end, and Max was as delighted as they were. 'I have given the poor things one happy hour,' he said."

TOURIST ON THE RHINE STEAMER.

Myrtle tossed her head scornfully, but I noticed that her eyes were kindly.

We have passed Stolzenfels — "The Castle of the Proud Rock." The Rhine from this point on bristles with castles and legends. The boat is lying now between the town of Kaub and the island of the Pfalz or Pfalz gräfenstein, crowned by a queer little many-turreted castle, formerly used as a toll-house. Louis the Debonair, the son of Charlemagne, died here.

This is really the most picturesque and historic part of the Rhine, and it amuses me to see how our fellow-passengers regard it. One grumpy old gentleman sits with his back to the scenery, eternally reading Bædecker. At the end of the trip he will know the name of every ruin, but he will not have seen any of them. A very pretty girl, who, I fancy, is an American, and who wears the most fascinating hats, at an average three different

KAUB AND THE PFALZ.

ones each day, flirts desperately with a clerical-appearing Heidelberg student.

Joe says he is sure he is a theological student, for that department is particularly addicted to pretty girls. "Do they study Byron?" I asked, as mischievously as I could; but Joe did not look in the least conscious, and Miss Boylston asked quietly, "Joe, who is the author of that sentimental bit about Drachenfels, which you always quote to every girl of your acquaintance?"

"That nonsense about the castled crags, and the little hand to hold? Murray, I suppose; at least, I found it in the guide-book."

We all laughed, and asked Joe how many times he had used the quotation.

"Not often," he replied; "you see English-speaking girls are rather scarce. I tried to translate it for the Countess, but when I reached the last line, she gave my hand such a grasp that she dislocated several of my metacarpal bones." Evidently, Joe was not as personal in his remarks as I supposed.

"Do be quiet, Joe," said Myrtle, against whom his light mood grated. "What sickening hats that girl wears!" she added, a few moments later.

"I do not find them so," I replied.

"No! when every one has at least three or four slaughtered birds on it?"

"But how pretty and jaunty; and you wear feathers yourself, Myrtle."

"Only ostrich plumes, and, since the times of ostrich-farming, the birds are not killed but cared for for their feathers. I would not wear that hat with twenty-seven humming-birds on it for any amount of money. Do you know, I read somewhere that one London dealer received a single consignment of thirty-two thousand dead humming-

birds, and another, at one time, thirty thousand aquatic birds and three hundred thousand pairs of wings. Mr. Gannet wrote a sweet little poem about it, and since then I have never worn a bird."

Myrtle took from her hand-bag a worn newspaper clipping, and read with real feeling: —

> Think what a price to pay,
> Faces so bright and gay.
> Just for a hat!
> Flower unvisited, mornings unsung,
> Sea-ranges bare of the wings that o'er swung,
> Bared just for that!
>
> Caught 'mid some mother work,
> Torn by a hunter Turk,
> Just for your hat!
> Plenty of mother-heart yet in the world,
> All the more wings to tear carefully twirled.
> *Women* want that?
>
> Oh, but the shame of it,
> Oh, but the blame of it, —
> Price of a hat!
> Just for a jauntiness brightening the street!
> This is your halo, O faces so sweet, —
> Death: and for that!

"Victoria studied taxidermy before we went to South America," I said, doubtfully, "and father approved of it, and there never was a kinder soul than he."

"That was in the cause of science, and yet I think that in its name very many cruel and unnecessary things have been done. I have a deep sympathy for every creature capable of suffering."

There was a look in Myrtle's eyes which seemed to say that this sympathy was itself born of suffering.

The attitude of the Colonel to his daughter is a strange one. They are more affectionate, but they do not look each other squarely in the face. The Colonel studies Myrtle furtively, and looks away when she glances up. He is continually pressing her with money, which she accepts and locks away in a little japanned tin box at the bottom of her trunk. "I do not need it now," she explained to me, "but it is well to be prepared for unforeseen exigencies."

This is so different from her old reckless, bountiful way. Does she think that she is a better guardian of the family fortune than her father, and it is well for her to keep all that she can lay hands on? And does the Colonel think that by this lavish generosity he excuses his own expenditures? It is all very sad and trying.

We are now at Bacharach, — the funniest old place that ever stepped out of theatrical scenery, the walls are so crazy, the roofs so steep, the façades of the houses criss-crossed with timbers like the lacing of some of the Swiss peasants' stockings.

Bacharach takes its name from *Bacchi ara*, altar of Bacchus, and it well sustains the name, and Longfellow's recommendation taken from the jingle of 1623: —

> "Zu Klingenberg am Main,
> Zu Würzburg an dem Stein,
> Zu Bacharach am Rhein,
> Hab' ich in meinen Tagen,
> Gar oftmals hören sagen,
> Soll'n sein die besten Wein."

The "altar" is a rock in the bed of the river. Pope Pius II. is said to have been so fond of Bacharach wine that a tun of it was sent him every year. We spent two days at Bacharach, climbing to the ruins of the castle of Stahlech on a hill behind the village, and visiting Werner's Church, fabled to contain the relics of the child Werner, falsely said to have been killed by the Jews. This is only one instance of the hate which the Germans in past centuries bore the Jews.

When the great Dresden porcelain works were founded at Meissen, Miss Boylston says that all Jews of a certain property were obliged to buy a quantity of the china pugs and shepherdesses, vases and statuettes, whether their taste lay in the way of this sort of bric-à-brac or not.   Indeed, their feelings were intentionally outraged, for they were obliged also to purchase the boars from the royal chase.

We read Longfellow's Golden Legend aloud last evening, and there was much that reminded us of this region.   Especially the old monk talking to the wine-casks in the cellar: —

> "Now here is a cask that stands alone.
> It comes from Bacharach on the Rhine,
> Is one of the three best kinds of wine,
> And costs some hundred florins the ohm;
> But that I do not consider dear,
> When I remember that every year
> Four butts are sent to the Pope of Rome;
> And whenever thereof a goblet I drain,
> The old rhyme keeps running in my brain:
> At Bacharach on the Rhine,
> At Hochheim on the Main,
> And at Würzburg on the Stein,
> Grow the three best kinds of wine.
>
> .   .   .   .
>
> See how its currents gleam and shine,
> As if they had caught the purple hues
> Of autumn sunsets on the Rhine,
> Descending and mingling with the dews:
> Or as if the grapes were stained with the blood
> Of the innocent boy who, some years back,
> Was taken and crucified by the Jews,
> In that ancient town of Bacharach;
> Perdition upon those infidel Jews,
> In that ancient town of Bacharach.
>
> .   .   .   .   .
>
> Here in the midst of the current I stand,
> Like the stone of Pfalz in the midst of the river,
> Taking toll upon either hand,
> And much more grateful to the giver."

It seems to me that a great deal too much poetry has been wasted upon wine.   Here, in the land of the grape, I had been told we would find less drunkenness than in America.   It is not true.   We have seen quite as much brawling over wine as one is likely to find

BACHARACH.

from American whiskey. A villanous crone, who held a bawling baby and begged at the street, alternately refreshed herself and the child from a can of genuine Bacharach wine.

After leaving Bacharach, we passed a succession of castles, and just before reaching Bingen, the Mouse Tower of Bishop Hatto. Southey's poem made such a vivid impression of terror upon me, as a child, and the vision of the wicked bishop pursued to his island castle and devoured by the rats has always seemed such an awful act of retributive justice, that I was

BEGGAR AT BACHARACH.

glad to find the whole legend regarded as mythical.

The Mausethurm, as it rises from the river, is a gloomy, sinister castle, which looks fully capable of enshrining a tragedy or a crime. Random lines from the ballad came to my memory; first, the burn-ing of the poor peasants enticed into the bishop's barns in the hope of receiving some of his grain:—

> " I' faith 'tis an excellent bonfire," quoth he;
> " And the country is greatly obliged to me
> For ridding it, in these times forlorn,
> Of rats that only consume the corn."

Then I seemed to hear the bishop's servant crying:—

> "Fly, my lord bishop, fly," quoth he,
> "Ten thousand rats are coming this way!
> The Lord forgive you for yesterday."
> "I'll go to my tower in the Rhine," replied he,
> " 'Tis the safest place in Germany;
> The walls are high, and the shores are steep,
> And the tide is strong, and the water deep."

Yes, I said to myself, if I had feared the rats, I think I should have thought myself safe there.

> "He laid him down and closed his eyes,
> But soon a scream made him arise.
>
> . . . . . .
>
> The cat sat screaming mad with fear
> At the army of rats that were drawing near;
> And in at the window, and in at the door,
> And through the walls, by thousands they pour;
> From within, from without, from above, from below,
> And all at once, to the bishop they go;
> They have whetted their teeth against the stones,
> And now they pick the bishop's bones,
> They gnawed the flesh from every limb,
> For they were sent to do judgment on him."

It is altogether a grewsome story, and I am glad it is not true. Joe is making a collection of the legends of the Rhine, and his version of them is quite amusing. The black hunters and headless horsemen, the stags with crosses for antlers, the little gnomes and ghostly maidens, laughing demons, angelic choirs, enchanted knights, and other dramatis personæ which he manages to weave into his stories, are mystifying to an ordinary intellect. He has one chapter devoted to appearances of the Evil One, with the bridges, and cliffs, and caves, named for him. He gathers his material not only from literature, but interrogates all our guides. I hear him chatting with a little fellow now, who has promised to take him to see a certain famous ruined tower.

AS HIGH AS A CHURCH SPIRE. "And every midnight there comes thereout a flame as high as a church spire." Joe is not at all incredulous; he has seen just as strange an appearance in his own country (a burning oil-well, presumably), where the evil demon

RÜDESHEIM.

issued not only at night, but in the day as well. He has engaged the slip of a boy to convey him to the dreadful spot. "But hold!" he says, "no flame, no money. The demon must get up his fireworks, or I shall consider it a base swindle."

At Bingen, Joe felt it necessary to allude to the "Soldier of the Legion, who lay dying at Algiers." He declaimed: —

> "I dreamed I stood with her, and saw the yellow sunlight shine
> On the vine-clad hills of Bingen, fair Bingen on the Rhine;
> I saw the blue Rhine sweep along; I heard, or seemed to hear,
> The German songs we used to sing in chorus sweet and clear;
> And her little hand lay lightly —"

Here we promptly extinguished him, having had quotations enough on this topic. Bingen is really a very pretty spot; we spent the night here, and in the morning crossed the river to Rüdesheim.

As we approached it, Myrtle started and exclaimed, "Look, Delight, there is the very castle from which the sketch was taken which affected me so on the ocean steamer."

Sure enough, here was the very battlemented tower which Myrtle had declared would have some strange influence on her life. "It is only the Brömersburg," Joe explained; "an

AT BINGEN ON THE RHINE.

old robber-castle of the thirteenth century. I do not fancy there are any of the band lurking within to harm you."

But Myrtle felt so strongly that she would not go over it, but remained with her father at a little inn near the river, while Miss Boylston, Joe, and I, made the somewhat windy ascent. The interior of the castle was rough in the extreme, the chambers smoke-blackened from great fires which the robbers had built here; but the view

from the roof repaid all our trouble.   Before us was extended the
Rheingau, the region from Rüdesheim to Mayence, the very Paradise
of the Rhine.

The Rhine spreads out here almost into a lake, and is filled with
innumerable islands and inlets, whose slopes are covered with vineyards, while the summits are crowned with ancient castles and
modern villas of the German nobility.   Skiffs and steam-yachts were
darting about among the islands, and flags were displayed from the
villas and the shipping.

We came down delighted with our view, and at last persuaded
Myrtle, since she would not enter the castle, at least to walk with us

AN UNEXPECTED MEETING.

to a little eminence from which the Rheingau was visible.   When
we had almost reached the spot, we saw that it was occupied; a
young German reclined at full length near the brink of the cliff, and
was looking away across the lovely landscape.   Myrtle caught my
arm, and would have led me back, but it was too late.   Joe bounded
forward and gave the unconscious tourist a resounding blow on the
shoulder, whereupon the assaulted man sprang to his feet, and the
two, instead of proceeding to blows, indulged in a hearty German
embrace.   Of course it was Mr. Blumenthal, who came toward us
smiling, with a glad light of triumph in his eyes.

"I have find you," he said, in his queer broken English.   "At
last, I am so happy as to have find you.   I am arrived at my mother's

the day after your departure. I take the cars to St. Goar, you are not yet arrive. I wait and wait, you come not; you probably do not stop by St. Goar, you are perhaps by Bacharach. I go to Bacharach, you make just to depart. I go to Lorch, I find you not. I come to Rüdesheim, the castle look at me so true, so kind as a friend. It say, wait, they will come here; wait, you shall yet find. 'Du solst noch einmal sehen.' That is what the river has been singing to me all the morning."

There were genuine tears in his good sentimental eyes. He was so thoroughly glad to see us all, so childlike in his confidence that we would be glad to see him. And we were glad, every one of us. The Colonel took one arm, Miss Boylston, who had known him a long time, the other; Joe gambolled about him like an excited dog. Myrtle walked a little apart, but she had greeted him with grave kindness; her eyes were downcast, but there were pleased little flickers about the mobile mouth. Yes, Myrtle was glad too.

CHAPTER X.

THE RHEINGAU. — MAYENCE. — SEVERAL CONVERSATIONS.

WE have taken a little yacht and boatman, who are to convey us along this lovely region as far as Mayence.

As we sit under the fluttering awning, the conversation is always general, and it is only when we pause to visit some ruin that the party breaks up into twos and threes, and there is any opportunity for confidences. At our first stop to visit the Schloss Johannisberg, it happened that Mr. Blumenthal was my escort. He was very interesting, for he told me the varied history of the castle; how a part of the building was a cloister of the Benedictines in 1106, how afterward it belonged to the Prince of Orange, William the Silent of the Netherlands, and later Marshal Kellermann received it as the gift of Napoleon, while in 1814 it became the property of Prince Von Metternich. The celebrated Johannisberg vineyards bring the family a princely income.

A pretty woman, picturesquely attired in what seemed to me rather a Tyrolese style, was walking on the terrace. She greeted us pleasantly, and gave us permission to pick some flowers. We wondered if she were a member of the family; gentle or simple, her manners were very sweet and gracious.

Mr. Blumenthal was not simply a cicerone. While we were viewing the pictures and statuary, he told me much about himself. He spoke of how grateful he was to Myrtle for having healed the family feud, and made peace for him with his mother.

"I haf long considered to myself," he confessed, "what we did talk about art, and I know myself now to haf been wrong; we could not be such friends as I did ask. She to gif me the inspiration of my paintings."

Ah! thought I, with delight, he is coming round to Myrtle's requirements. She is not to serve him, but he will serve her; when suddenly my gratification was thrown into confusion by his next remark.

"I haf thought it ofer, I could not take her help; I cannot be a great painter of history and of imagination. I haf my own work, which is more little, but which is mine own; that work I must do, and nobody can help me."

I was startled. How would such independence as this strike Myrtle? For myself, I rather liked it. Mr. Blumenthal seemed to me more of a man than ever before. Joe and he are very unlike, and yet Joe is not so flippant as he seems. We walked back from the villa to the boat together, and he said, very gravely, "Miss Holmes, you are a very intimate friend of my sister, and I presume you know the trouble which is weighing on her mind, — her fears about father."

"Yes," I replied. "I have guessed them, and I am glad to see that you do not share them."

THE LADY OF
THE VILLA.

"Ah, but I do," he answered, "though I would not have her know it for the world. I laugh it off with her, and conduct myself generally like a mountebank or a court fool, to try to tempt her out of her Castle of Despair. I presume now you have given me the credit of being a vapid, brainless apology for a man, but I assure you that I have my pretty serious moments, when I wonder what is to be the outcome of all this. Still, I believe that we children ought not to be wholly crushed by the legacies of past generations. I know that I have escaped the

love of gaming, and I try to hearten myself, as well as poor Myrtle, by my weak attempts at gayety."

We spoke of Mr. Blumenthal, and Joe agreed with me that Myrtle and he seemed to be drifting apart. He has obtained several quiet walks with her, after each of which she has seemed to grow more and more serious.

THE WALK THROUGH THE VINEYARD.

We are at Mayence now, and I have one more conversation to chronicle. We had moored the little craft to attend church one Sabbath at a pretty little chapel. Myrtle placed her arm in mine as we set out, and the others paired off in various ways.

"And again we have a picture from the Golden Legend," I said, —

MAYENCE.

"The swift and mantling river
Flows on triumphant through these lovely regions
As when the vanguard of the Roman legions
First saw it from the top of yonder hill!
How beautiful it is!   Fresh fields of wheat,
Vineyard, and town, and tower with fluttering flag,
The consecrated chapel on the crag,
And the white hamlet gathered round its base,
Like Mary sitting at her Saviour's feet,
And looking up at his beloved face!"

But Myrtle did not reply, and, pressing her arm closer, I said, "You are looking so very sad that I cannot keep silence. What is the matter, Myrtle dear?"

"The trouble is this," she said quietly: "Mr. Blumenthal wishes me to marry him."

"I am sure I do not see anything so very lugubrious in that," I replied. "I am sorry he does not appreciate what a help you would be in directing his painting, but perhaps you can bring him to understand."

"That has nothing to do with the case," Myrtle replied, impatiently. "I am glad he has found that he can work alone. He does not need me for his art, but I believe that he loves me truly, and he is so true, so simple-hearted, so noble and good, that it would be an honor for any woman to be loved by such a man."

"Then why do you not accept him?" I asked. "You know you love him; your brother is his sworn friend; you like his mother and sister, and I think your father approves."

"You have touched the painful spot," she said, frankly. "My father! How can I marry any man and overwhelm him in our family ruin?"

"You fear that your father's fondness for gaming is unconquerable?"

"If he could rob me of my dead mother's jewels to pay a gambling debt!"

"You have no proof that he has done so," I replied.

"I have every proof, and I feel our present disgrace so deeply that when it is known to every one I shall not suffer any more. To every one but Mr. Blumenthal; I cannot bear to tell him, and yet I must, for he insists on knowing why I will not listen to him."

We entered the church and heard a sermon in German, which we could not entirely understand. During its progress some one in the choir recognized Miss Boylston and took her up to the organ-loft. Presently we saw that she was playing, leading the congregational singing in that grand old hymn of Luther's which Prince Leopold called "God's Dragoon March," "Eine feste Burg ist unser Gott."

Myrtle caught the spirit; she was not comforted or soothed, but carried away, as it were, by the swing and spirit of a marching host, and was ready to go with them to victory or death. As we walked back to the boat together, I said to her, "I can see that you have decided to tell him all."

"No, not to tell him, for then he would feel obliged to protest that it made no difference,— to match my confession by a grand unselfishness; but I shall place him in a position where he can see everything, where he will think that he has discovered it himself, and you shall see he will gladly accept the easy retreat which I will offer him. As soon as we reach Mayence, father has decided to leave us in the city for a day or two, and make a little trip to Wiesbaden alone. I shall arrange to have Mr. Blumenthal go with him."

"But there is no longer any gaming at Wiesbaden," I replied, quite puzzled. "The government has closed all the gambling-houses."

"Of course, there are no public ones; but you may be sure there are plenty of private opportunities; and, Delight, I have ascertained a bit of information. Mr. Van Bergen is at Wiesbaden. Father received a letter at Bingen. I did not read it, but I saw the postmark, and knew the hand."

"I am glad Mr. Blumenthal is going with your father," I replied; "but are you sure that you can manage it?"

It ended as Myrtle had planned. The Colonel and Mr. Blumenthal went away this morning over the bridge of boats to Castel, on the opposite bank of the river, from which point the railroad will bring them in twenty minutes to Wiesbaden.

The rest of us, having the city on our hands, went, as was our duty, this morning, to see the cathedral. I think it contains the greatest jumble of different styles of architecture of any edifice I have ever seen. It is remarkable in another way also — for its tombs. Like the Catacombs, it is walled and paved with them. A great many are of archbishops. Joe says it must have been very distressing to the stone-cutters to play a new variation each time on the same theme. He thinks it must have been almost as trying as to think up a new way of writing a valedictory. Thorwaldsen's statue of Gutenberg, the inventor of printing, who was born in Mayence, stands near the

ART STUDENT NO. I.

cathedral. After this we visited a picture-gallery, where several students were copying old masters. Joe carried the camera and made instantaneous pictures. One of the students was an elderly man, with bald head, and spectacles, but his work was very young indeed.

At one church a fee to the sacristan gave permission for Miss Boylston to use the organ. Joe pumped, and she gave us the Andante from the 5th Symphony, and the Descent of the Holy Grail, from "Lohengrin." Then she talked with us of her ideas of sacred

music, her memories of church choirs and congregational singing in
America, the greater devotional spirit put into church music in Germany, and her intention to go back to America soon to try somewhere to institute a little reform. "I think I can get a position as
organist in some small church," she said; "then if I can only im-
press my choir with a sense that music is worship! When I remember the flirtations that I have seen carried on in organ-lofts, between
the soprano and the tenor, while the alto writes notes on the blank
leaves of the hymnal, and the whispering and giggling is hardly in-

termitted during prayer, my very soul is
sick. The most sublime hymns are rattled
off with no conception of their meaning.
The basso sings at a comic opera during
the week. The organist plays popular
airs as interludes. The congregation does
not care; it regards its music as so much
decoration, like the cheap frescoing spread
over as much space and with as gaudy
effect as possible."

"Do you think congregational singing
would be better?" Myrtle asked.

"Far better, provided the organist were
capable of leading. An organist should
understand music structurally, its analysis

ART STUDENT NO. 2.

and composition, should have capacity for expressing emotion, and a
knowledge of the powers of the human voice. St. Ann's is a good
example of tunes adapted for congregational singing, and there are
many plain songs which run in moderate compass, neither high nor
low, which have a grand effect when sung by a mixed multitude. I
must say, however, that I am very partial to children's voices. I
should form a choir of them, for certain parts of the service. This is
the end to which I intend to devote my musical studies."

" I thought," said Joe, " that you had already achieved success in musical composition, and were going to compose operas."

" Doubtless, there is a reform needed in that direction also," said Miss Boylston, with a smile; " but at present I think that church music is really worse than operatic."

Next morning the Colonel and Mr. Blumenthal returned from Wiesbaden. I watched them anxiously, and was not reassured by their manner. The Colonel seemed plunged in profound gloom. He rarely spoke, and it was necessary to address him twice to obtain an answer to a question. Mr. Blumenthal, on the contrary, was more chatty than is his wont; he described

LOOKING AT THE ANIMALS.

Wiesbaden, and regretted that we had not visited it also. He had much to say of the springs, the lovely gardens, the residences of the nobility, and, above all, of the lovely children. "Ah!" said he, "we saw at the *Thiergarten* some such heavenly beautiful ones, I greatly regretted not to have brought my sketch-box."

Not a word did he say, however, of whether any gaming-places were open, nor that the Colonel had quite by chance met an old friend, a certain Mr. Van Bergen; but for all that, Myrtle, Joe, and I were perfectly certain that they had met, and played, and that the Colonel had lost heavily.

CHAPTER XI.

HEIDELBERG. — BROKEN TOWERS AND UNITED HEARTS.

I WONDER if there is in all the world a more enchanting spot than Heidelberg. The town rises in terraces from the Neckar to the Castle, and above the Castle again tower the Geisberg Mountains. Fascinating walks, or rather climbs, tempt us on every hand; and however beautiful may be the view where you happen to be, you are told that one far finer is to be obtained from a point just beyond.

We took the steamer from Mayence to Manheim, and then turned from the Rhine to explore the Neckar for about fifteen miles, when this vision of loveliness burst upon us.

We decided to visit the Castle before the University. If I am to be disappointed in my hope of obtaining lessons here, I will put off the evil day as far as possible, and not lose the sense of proprietorship which is so pleasant as you explore the ins and outs of a charming place which may possibly be your home. We are not a gay party just now, but the delicious air, the enchanting scenery, and the glorious weather, could not fail to cheer the saddest.

We found that the town consisted of one main street about three miles long. We mounted the hill to the celebrated castle so long the residence of the Palatine Elector and Counts who kept in order the bandit nobles of the Odenwald and the Neckar, the Counts who were little more than highwaymen, the ruins of whose castles crown every hill and dominate every pass. Heidelberg Castle is a beautiful ruin. It was destroyed by the French in 1688, but the walls still stand, with their fine carvings, showing the various styles of the dif-

HEIDELBERG CASTLE FROM THE TERRACE.

ferent periods in which it was erected. We descended into a cellar to see the famous tun, thirty-six feet long and twenty-four feet high, with a capacity of eight hundred hogsheads, a suggestive relic of a hard drinking age. Myrtle took several photographs of the imposing ruin, and then we visited the better preserved portions and wandered down the terrace into the garden. I passed Mr. Blumenthal as he was leaning on the parapet and looking sadly away toward the lovely Neckar, and heard him repeating softly to himself a poem by Heine : —

> "Es ist eine alte Geschichte,
>   Und geht nichts grosses dabei ;
> Doch wem es eben passiret,
>   Dem bricht das Herz entzwei."

Freely translated, this may signify that it's an old story and not of much consequence, but his heart is breaking. "Yes," I said, "it is enough to break one's heart to see this magnificent building so wantonly destroyed." But I knew that he was not thinking of the Castle.

As we returned to the hotel for luncheon, we passed by some of

STUDENTS.

the buildings of the University, the Anatomical and Zoölogical Museums. Our hotel is very near the Botanical Garden, and I shall profit by it for a little study. We saw numbers of the students in the streets, some sitting at little tables in the beer-gardens, absorbing vast quantities of Rhine wine. Many of them wore society caps, which gave them a military appearance, as did the patches and scars which told of duelling encounters. I remarked to Joe that they looked more like soldiers than students, and he replied: "You will have to

take fencing lessons if you settle here. As soon as it is known that you are a student of the University, you will be deluged with challenges to duels, and no one will ever believe that you have studied at Heidelberg, unless you can show half a dozen sword-cuts, an ear or two clipped, a slice off your nose, or a seam across your forehead."

"I shall pusillanimously decline all my challenges," I laughed; and Joe shook his head, declaring I would never do for Heidelberg. After luncheon we acted on a suggestion of Myrtle's to make an excursion to Neckar-Steinach, and eat a picnic supper in one of the old ruined castles, returning on the river by moonlight. We made the trip in a little sailboat. From the river, the castle seemed inaccessible on its nearly perpendicular cliff, but our guide led us around the point, and we found the ascent not over-difficult. Myrtle easily took the lead, leaping from rock to rock like a frisky young chamois, often quite out of sight. Mr. Blumenthal was a little piqued that she should outstrip him, but he was burdened with the camera and the Colonel's telescope, beside being kept back by a desire to be polite to Miss Boylston and myself. After a time he left us, and, taking a short cut up the face of the cliff, joined Myrtle just as she reached the castle wall. This is the highest and oldest ruin in the valley; it is called Swallow's-nest, and innumerable black wings were fluttering about the high towers, just as at grandfather's homestead, in Massachusetts, the swallows settle at sunset into the great chimney.

I found some harebells and picked them for my herbarium.

"Do you remember Mrs. Howitt's poem to the Harebell?" Miss Boylston asked. I was obliged to confess that I did not, and she repeated it for me: —

> The very flower to take
> .Into the heart and make
> The cherished memory of all pleasant places;
> Name but the light harebell,
> And straight is pictured well
> Where'er of fallen state lie lonely traces.

ENTRANCE TO HEIDELBERG CASTLE.

Old slopes of pasture ground;
Old fosse, and moat, and mound,
Where the mailed warrior and crusader came:
Old walls of crumbling stone
Where trails the snap-dragon;
Rise at the speaking of the harebell's name.

"There is a wayside cross," said the Colonel, "where the mailed warrior and crusader might appear as very suitable adjuncts to the landscape."

"I fancy if they did appear," grumbled Joe, who was groaning under the lunch-basket, "that we might be invited to make a longer visit at the dungeon-keep, up there, than we would care to. They were gay old cocks of the loft, and extended a sort of hospitality to tourists like ourselves which was hard to resist."

When we reached the castle, we found Myrtle and Mr. Blu-

MAILED WARRIORS.

menthal deep in conversation; evidently it was nothing of a romantic nature, but something of deep and grave importance, for Mr. Blu-

menthal looked troubled, and Myrtle was strangely excited; she seemed glad, and yet afraid to be glad. She started up and met her father, as we approached, with such a keen questioning glance, in which hope and love, doubt and self-reproach, were all strangely mingled. I could not understand it. I only felt sure that they had been talking of the Colonel, and that there were some new developments. Myrtle was a little distrait throughout the charming time, for all that. Joe built a bonfire in the courtyard, and we gathered about it while the coffee boiled and the apples roasted, and told ghost stories, and the fairy legends which the Germans love, of the Lorelei and Kobolds and elfin sprites. Even the Colonel contributed his part, repeating Bulwer's Song of the Fairies in the ruins of Heidelberg: —

> From the woods and the glossy green
>   With the wild thyme strewn ;
> From the river whose crisped sheen
>   Is kissed by the trembling moon ;
> While the dwarf looks out from his mountain cave,
>   And the erl king from his lair,
> And the water-nymph from her moaning wave,
>   We skirr the limber air.
> There's a smile on the vine-clad shore,
>   A smile on the castled heights ;
> They dream back the days of yore,
>   And they smile at our roundel rites,
>   Our roundel rites !
> Lightly we tread these halls around.
>   Lightly tread we ;
> Yet, hark ! we have scared with a single sound
> The moping owl on the breathless tree,
>   And the goblin sprites !
> Ha ! ha ! we have scared with a single sound
> The gray old owl on the breathless tree,
>   And the goblin sprites.

It happened that as the Colonel finished his recitation an owl did hoot, whereat we all shrieked or laughed, and the walls echoed the

CASTLE OF NECKAR-STEINACH.

sound quite dismally. The light of our fire must have flared out through the loopholes, and perhaps the peasants below thought us the phantoms of the old robber counts come back again to light their baleful beacons and revel with demoniac laughter in the old halls.

Myrtle tapped at my door very early the next morning, and asked me if I would not like to walk to the terrace before breakfast, and

HEIDELBERG TERRACE.

there, looking away over the lovely landscape, she told me what had moved her so strongly the evening before. I will give it in her own language: —

"Mr. Blumenthal said that he wished to speak to me for a moment, of something which he thought I ought to know, as it concerned me deeply. I was sure that he meant father's fondness for cards, especially as he said that it was something that had come to his knowledge at Wiesbaden, and had made him very unhappy. I said to myself: This is just what I expected would happen; he is going to tell me that he is very sorry for me, etc., but that he could never think of uniting his fortunes with a gambler's daughter. So I steeled myself to listen to it, and was trying to think just what I would reply, when the story took such a different turn from what I had expected, that I was struck speechless with astonishment. It seems that on the way to Wiesbaden father had confided to Mr. Blumenthal that he wished to meet a Mr. Van Bergen on business of a private nature, but that he was glad to have Mr. Blumenthal with him, as he wished a witness to their interview, and he would rather trust him in a confidential matter than any one whom he knew. All this was quite as I expected; but now comes the remarkable part. When they met Mr. Van Bergen, father charged him with having advanced me money on my diamond cross, and insisted on his returning the jewels at once. Think of it! all this time I had believed that father had sold the cross to Mr. Van Bergen, and here was father harboring the same notion in regard to me! Mr. Van Bergen denied the entire matter, and demanded the proofs of father's suspicions. These he could not give, and they had quite an angry quarrel, which might have come to something serious, if Mr. Blumenthal had not separated them and got father away.

"That night father told Mr. Blumenthal the whole story from his standpoint. He spoke of the family tendency toward extravagance, which he feared I had inherited, of his own passion for play, which he averred he had strangled for my sake, declaring that he had not played for money since we made our compact at Waterloo, and had touched cards at all but once at Cologne, where he happened to meet this Mr. Van Bergen. He gave me the credit of having kept my part of the contract too, until we had seen Mr. Blumenthal's picture at Bonn, when, rather than apply for the money which he would willingly have given me, he believed I had pawned my cross to Mr. Van Bergen. He had been led to think so because Mr. Van Bergen had spoken of the jewels at Cologne, and had said that he intended sending me some photographs of new ways of setting jewels. All this father told Mr. Blumenthal that he ought to know, for it might make a difference in his feelings towards me. And the best of it all was, Delight, that it had not. Mr. Blumenthal told me all in the gentlest, most respectful manner. 'I feel sure,' he said, in his broken English, 'sure there was some mistake, and so I told your father. I knew Miss Boujoulac could not make it possible to deceive. If she had wish to sell her jewels, it would be all right,—I have nothing to say to that, — but she would not sell in so disprincipled a way.' Then he assured father that I never could have cared for a picture of his sufficiently to have bought it, and that his own mother had purchased the picture of which he spoke. 'It is all one horrible mistake,' he said again, 'but I beg of you to explain to your father so much of it as you can.'"

"That is it," I interrupted; "all this trouble has come, Myrtle, because you have not confided in your father; let there be perfect frankness and truth between you, and all will be explained."

"I don't know about that," Myrtle replied, thoughtfully. "I certainly shall talk it all over with father, and we will believe in each other; but that will not explain the disappearance of the cross. Mr. Blumenthal says that all the servants at the rittergut are irreproachably honest, and have been in the family for years. He thinks that I may have lost it there, and wishes to write his mother to institute a thorough search. I asked him to wait until father and I had had our confessions. We will have our opportunity to-day. Father, true to his military instincts, wishes to inspect a tower which has been blown up by a mine. I will go with him, if you will take the rest of the party with you to visit the University."

It was late at night when we reached our hotel, but still later we heard bands of strolling students, now by twos and threes, and now in a full männerchor, singing the "Landesvater" and other songs in honor of love, wine, their fatherland, or their University. The songs, tempered by distance, mingled with our dreams like delightful serenades, but I could not help wishing that the students were a little less rollicking, and more gentlemanly.

LATER.

It is all over. My dream of studying at Heidelberg is at an end. We have called to-day at the house of one of the professors. He was absent, and we were entertained by the Frau Professorin and her granddaughter, a perkish little maid in a broad hat, who listened

demurely to our conversation, and reflected the varying expressions on her grandmother's face, especially the blank astonishment which greeted my announcement of my wish to settle in Heidelberg and study at the University. "*Gott bewahr!*" It was impossible! "*Eine Fräulein student!*" it was "*wunderbar*" and "*unerhört!*" not to say "*shrecklich!*"

And yet she was a woman of intelligence and some education.

THE FRAU PROFESSORIN AND HER
GRANDDAUGHTER.

She had been busy mounting specimens for her husband's herbarium, when we entered, labelling them very neatly. I drew her attention to this. Oh, yes, she had studied at a convent in Strasburg, and her husband had taught her more since they had married.

"You see," said Joe, as we left, "the only way for you to get instruction is to marry one of these old professors; then it will be all right. How shocked the old lady was at your shameful and unmaidenly desire to know something about ferns. I really feel mortified to have been seen in your company."

I was deeply disappointed, and had it not been for Joe's chaff, I

RUINS OF A CASTLE.

fear I would have broken down and cried. Joe proposed a walk to the Wolfsbrunnen and to the Königstuhl, a height behind the castle, from which it is said the Strasburg Cathedral can be seen. The walk did me good, though we saw nothing of the famous spires. I thought of the words " On every height there lies repose," and was calmed and strengthened.

The Colonel and Myrtle joined us on our return to the hotel. It seemed to me that they each looked ten years younger, and I solaced myself, in my own chagrin and defeat, by the look of radiant trust and happiness in their faces. Nothing was said, however, of the confidences which had passed between them, — of doubts confessed and faith renewed. Myrtle was silent, and the Colonel talked volubly of the broken tower which they had been to see, — a tower about two hundred years old when it was blown up; but so firmly was the rock cemented that all that war could do was to split it in halves, one mass falling on its side, and the other still standing and defying the centuries to destroy it.

"That was wonderful cement," said the Colonel. "I wish we could invent something like it."

Ah, I thought, your heart and Myrtle's are cemented together at last, so that no dynamite of doubt can ever divide them.

CHAPTER XII.

THE BLACK FOREST.

WE decided to make the trip from Heidelberg to Strasburg by the railroad which runs through the northern portion of the Schwarzwald, or Black Forest.

The villages which we see from the car-windows are very picturesque; the houses having timbered fronts, and queer galleries and balconies.

Our first stop was, at Carlsruhe, a sufficiently stupid town, named from the fact that the Margrave Charles of Baden-Durlach built a hunting-lodge here when all around was wilderness and forest. Baden we found more interesting. It is the most fashionable watering-place of Germany, and is sometimes called Baden Baden, to imply that here are the *Baden*, or Baths, *par excellence*, and to distinguish it from other Badens. It is said that at the height of the season there are not unfrequently fifty thousand strangers in the place. The estimate sounds preposterous, but it is probably correct. We visited the Conversationshaus the evening of our arrival, and the next morning explored the dungeons under the Castle. These are very extensive, and were possibly the judgment-hall, dungeons, and chambers of torture of some secret tribunal. We were shown a rusty thumbscrew, and dropped some pebbles into an oubliette into which poor wretches were thrown. We heard the pebbles bound and rebound for nearly a quarter of a minute, and the faint splash which told that there was water at the bottom. We were glad to escape from this ghastly place into the bright little schnecken-garten, where snails were formerly raised for the princely table.

A VILLAGE IN THE BLACK FOREST.

There are ruins of old Roman baths here, which told that the hot springs were known and used in very ancient times.

Princes of the blood, dukes, and duchesses were dashing about in elegant equipages. Mr. Blumenthal found some friends stopping at the hotel which he had chosen, among others a Count, a distinguished-appearing man, who has been most polite. There is a pretty little kiosk at the end of the terrace, and Myrtle and I were carrying our journals and letters there this morning, when we noticed that it was already occupied. The Count sat with his back toward the entrance, holding in his hand a pack of cards. He was speaking to some one whom we could not see, and his words were very clear and distinct.

"But, Herr Colonel," he said, "a quiet little game like this, low stakes, — where's the harm? It passes the time, we are secure from observation, no one is the wiser."

Myrtle gasped, and leaned on me heavily. I thought she would faint. Poor girl, she had been through so much, and was so happy at Heidelberg in her ather's promises, that now I pitied her. But in a moment the Colonel's answer came: —

THE COUNT.

"I thank you, Herr Graf, but, even if there were no stakes, I must decline your invitation. I have sworn never to touch a card again, and by God's help I will keep the resolution."

Myrtle seized my hand and drew me quickly away. Her father had stood as severe a test as could probably be given him, and she had now good ground for her confidence.

Later in the morning we saw from our window the Colonel seated on a garden bench reading the Zeitung. "Is he not noble?" Myrtle cried. "Is he not exactly your conception of a hero? How grand he is!" and, catching up her hat, she hastily joined him. As I looked at the Colonel, I could not help smiling; the broad Panama hat bore little resemblance to a knightly helmet, and his long, lank legs reminded me of no hero of history unless it were Don Quixote, and yet I felt, with Myrtle, that there was something heroic in the man who could so conquer himself. He drew Myrtle tenderly to his side, and the peasant woman and little girl with her hair braided in two tails who sat behind them discreetly withdrew, evidently under the impression that here was a wedded pair in the early part of their honeymoon. I think that the consciousness that each has wronged the other in thought, and that they have each been fully forgiven, is the deepest cause of their grateful happiness. Some one has said that there is no joy which so penetrates the depths of the soul as that which flows from a sense of unmerited

THE COLONEL.

grace; and this must be the feeling of every one who comes into true relations with his Heavenly Father.

We are now at Oberkirch, a quaint little village where musical boxes, and the wood-carvings for which the Black Forest is so celebrated, are made by the peasants.

We came to Oberkirch in this way. I am especially interested in peasants, and, after leaving Baden, in order to see more of them, Joe and I rode to the next stopping-place, Achern, in a third-class car, and I was greatly amused by the types which presented themselves. They were not all peasants, however. There was one grocer's wife and some other small shopkeepers; Joe chatted with them for my benefit. When he told the grocer's lady that we were Americans, she raised her hands in horror. "And where are your other wives?" she asked of Joe. We did not understand the drift

PEASANT'S HOUSE IN THE BLACK FOREST.

of her remark at first, but it afterwards transpired that a Mormon elder had been preaching in her village, and she was under the impression that all Americans were polygamists. I asked if the elder made many converts, and it seemed that he had carried away fifty or more. It is astonishing that our government will permit the entrance of these poor deluded creatures, who are imported from all parts of

Europe to feed the great evil, which is spreading itself to our shame and peril.

Achern is interesting only from the quaintness of its houses, and for being the point of departure for the ruined Abbey of Allerheiligen, or All Saints. We accordingly hired a sort of omnibus or diligence, painted like a circus band-wagon, with a postilion to match, who smokes a meerschaum pipe and wears a Tyrolese hat, and were off by a delightful road between the dark pine-clad hills to the Abbey.

THE POSTILION.

We were all in such high spirits that no one would have recognized us for the dejected party of the Rheingau. Myrtle and Mr. Blumenthal have come to a complete understanding, and their happiness is contagious. There seems to be nothing in the way of their union, and there is to be a formal betrothal, in the old German style, at his sister's house at Munich, where we are to betake ourselves when we have finished our Rhine trip. Mr. Blumenthal has written his mother begging her to meet us there, and has no doubt that she will do so, for a betrothal in Germany is a very important event. He has also written her about the lost cross, and we hope to hear from her at Strasburg.

We found Allerheiligen Abbey a little gem; it reminded me of an artificial ruin built for effect in a gentleman's garden, it was so studiedly graceful; Mr. Blumenthal took out his color-box and made a sketch of it, while the postilion rehearsed the legend of its building, so fluently as to lead us to suspect that this was possibly the one-thousandth repetition. It was founded by an unhappy woman, the Duchess Uta Von Schauenberg, whose worthless husband having left

RUINS OF THE ABBEY OF ALLERHEILIGEN.

her a widow, she, in pure thankfulness, determined to found an abbey. For some strange reason, the site of the proposed edifice was left to a donkey. The funds were placed in its panniers, and it was allowed to roam at will, until, tired of its burden, it rolled upon the ground, and, emptying its panniers, plainly showed to the duchess and her priestly attendants, who were following, that this was the chosen spot.

Miss Boylston expressed surprise at this proceeding, but Joe insisted that it was a delicate compliment on the part of the widow to her deceased husband. As she could not consult him in the matter, she referred the choice to a representative resembling him as nearly as possible in manners and intelligence.

We were so much pleased with what we had seen of the Black Forest that we asked the postilion if there was not some village where we could spend the night, instead of returning over the same route to Achern, and the man spoke in such terms of Oberkirch that we determined to visit it. We arrived late at night, and not a little tired of our jaunt. The inn to

DORTCHEN.

which our postilion brought us was a comfortable one, but we soon saw why the rogue was so anxious to bring us around this way. He was thinking not so much of our interests as of Dortchen, the inn-keeper's pretty barefooted daughter. She reminded us of Auerbach's Barfüssle, and we remembered that Auerbach was born in the Black Forest, and that many of his stories of village life were

laid here. Dortchen showed us with pride the cherry-trees at the back of the house, and the pots of preserves which she had made this season. We have remained here several days, and have had no reason to regret our coming. Sunday there was a Gottesdienst, or festival, at the village church, and Monday was a Feiertag, or market-day, when the peasants gathered in from all the country round. We bought a number of souvenirs; Miss Boylston, a crucifix carved in wood, and I some boxes of wooden toys, Noah's arks, and villages with the funny stiff trees. These had all been carved at home, the youngest children shaping the animals and houses, and painting the hyenas green and the giraffes pink, according to their very original ideas of Zoölogy. I shall bring these toys back with me for some children whom I know in America. Myrtle saw a cuckoo-clock which she coveted, but she examined her little account-book carefully, and did not buy it.

These Germans are very industrious and ingenious; some one has called them the Yankees of Europe. What vigor and manhood the Teutonic race has shown, in fighting first Cæsar, then the Pope, and lastly the Napoleons! There are stamina here and an honesty of purpose, with a certain noble simplicity which we, with all our boasted refinement, might well cultivate.

Something a little startling has happened here. Myrtle has developed a tendency to sleep-walking, which she possessed when a child, but supposed she had entirely outgrown. A long balcony runs outside of our window. It reminded us, when we first saw it, of the one at the rittergut, especially as it contained some boxes of flowers. Last night I was awakened by Myrtle's opening the window and stepping out upon this gallery. It flashed through my mind at once that she must be walking in her sleep, and, greatly alarmed, for I had no idea what she might do in such a state, I threw a wrapper about me and followed her. She walked the length of the gallery, and began pulling up the flowers which were planted in the boxes. She kept at the work with a good deal of spirit, only stopping when she had uprooted every plant; when she turned and walked back to our room, passing me with wide-staring eyes. I stopped to replace the

OBERKIRCH.

poor plants, and, when I returned to the room, found her sleeping quietly. I talked over the occurrence with her this morning, and she could scarcely believe that she had returned to the old habit, until the earth on her hands convinced her. The strangest part of the freak is that we cannot think of anything which could have suggested this sudden passion for gardening. We were talking, just before we retired, of the unexplained mystery surrounding the loss of her diamond cross. " Perhaps," said Joe, " you fancied you were in Brazil digging for diamonds. I hope you will tie yourself to Miss Holmes after this every night, as it is not at all pleasant to know that we have a somnambulist in the party who may take a fancy that my head is a cocoa-nut which needs cracking."

In spite of Joe's trifling, it is a serious matter. Myrtle thinks that she may have had her tulip in mind, which has lately been quite forgotten. She unearthed it from the depths of the lunch-basket, where it had been crushed under a jar of Black Forest cherries of Dortchen's preserving, watered it, and placed it in the sun, but I fear it is quite dead.

We leave Oberkirch to-morrow for Strasburg, via the little towns of Appenweir and Kehl. Our stay has been in the northern half of the Black Forest; after leaving Strasburg, we will traverse the southern portion, on our way to Lake Constance.

CHAPTER XIII.

STRASBURG. — WAR MEMORIES. — TWO ARCHITECTS.

MISS BOYLSTON has some friends in Strasburg who are partly French, at least in their sympathies. They were formerly wealthy, but since the war have become reduced in circumstances, and keep a *pension*, or boarding-house. We wrote to them from Baden, and received an answer stating that they would be happy to entertain us.

The family consists of Madame Hautcœur, and her two daughters, Marguérite and Gabrielle.

Of course the chief object of interest in Strasburg is the Cathedral, and we were glad to find that the Hautcœurs live almost under its shadow. We could hardly wait for luncheon before we sallied out to see it. Mademoiselle Marguérite offered to go with us as guide. She is a stylish young person, handsome but for a scar on her left cheek. She wears such a high steeple hat that Joe remarked, *sotto voce*, that he felt sure it was modelled after the tower of the Cathedral.

Marguérite's feeling for the Germans, is very much like the Southerner's opinion of the Yankees, and Mr. Blumenthal wisely kept himself in the background. Strasburg is fast becoming a German city, but there are still many French residents, who cherish bitter feelings against their conquerors, and feel that Alsace ought to belong to France. Both French and Germans are proud and fond of the Cathedral, and rightly so, for it is one of the finest in Europe. During the siege, the Germans only once directed their fire toward the Cathedral, and this was because the French commander had made the platform a signal station and place of observation. Even then, the shells were sent with such precision that they passed directly over the platform without scathing the tower.

The spire is the highest in the world, four hundred and sixty-six feet, several feet higher than the great pyramid of Cheops.

PLATFORM OF STRASBURG CATHEDRAL.

Its clock is a wonder of mechanism. The hours are struck by a figure of Death. In an upper recess stands a statue of Christ, and at noon the twelve apostles march out and bow before him.

We mounted to the platform of the lower tower, where we obtained a magnificent view of the city, of the Rhine, and the Black Forest. We could trace the water communications of the city, which are remarkable, as it is connected "by the Rhine with the North Sea; by the Marne and Seine with the English Channel; by the Saone and Rhone with the Mediterranean; and by the Louis Canal, the Main, and the Danube, with the Black Sea." With these

STRASBURG CATHEDRAL.

four outlets for traffic, it is no wonder that it is one of the most
important commercial centres in the interior of Europe. It is connected with the four waterways mentioned by the smaller river Ill
and by numerous canals, which make the city a German Venice.

Queer steep-roofed old houses are built by the sides of the canals,
with sheds projecting over the water, where the laundresses wash
their linen.

A STREET IN STRASBURG.

After enjoying for a long time the extensive view, and asking a
few questions of the watchmen who are stationed here to look out
for fire, we descended to the interior of the Cathedral, which Longfellow describes so well in the Golden Legend. Elsie entering
exclaims: —

"How very grand it is and wonderful!
Never have I beheld a church so splendid!
Such columns, and such arches, and such windows,
So many tombs and statues in the chapels,
And under them so many confessionals.
They must be for the rich. I should not like
To tell my sins in such a church as this.
Who built it?"

Prince Henry replies: —

> "A great master of his craft,
>   Erwin von Steinbach; but not he alone,
>   For many generations labored with him.
>   Children that came to see these Saints in stone,
>   As day by day out of the blocks they rose,
>   Grew old and died, and still the work went on,
>   And on, and on, and is not yet completed.
>   The generation that succeeds our own
>   Perhaps may finish it.   The architect
>   Built his great heart into these sculptured stones,
>   And with him toiled his children, and their lives
>   Were builded with his own into the walls
>   As offerings unto God.   You see that statue
>   Fixing its joyous but deep wrinkled eyes
>   Upon the pillar of the Angels yonder?
>   That is the image of the master, carved
>   By the fair hand of his own child, Sabina.
>
> *Elsie.*
> How beautiful is the column that he looks at!
>
> *Prince Henry.*
> That, too, she sculptured.   At the base of it
> Stand the Evangelists; above their heads
> Four Angels blowing upon marble trumpets,
> And over them the blessed Christ, surrounded
> By his attendant ministers upholding
> The instruments of his Passion."

We found it all as Longfellow has so beautifully pictured it, and I think all our hearts silently cried with Elsie: —

> "O my Lord!
> Would I could leave behind me upon earth,
> Some monument to thy glory such as this."

The Cathedral was begun in 1015 by Erwin of Steinbach, the work was carried on by his son, and his daughter Sabina, who deserves to be remembered as one of the first women who succeeded grandly as an architect, and was completed by John Stultz of Cologne in 1601.

The front of the Cathedral is an intricate tracery of lace-work in stone. Myrtle said it reminded her of a bride looking through her veil. We saw it by daylight with every detail of carving illuminated, but I would like also to visit it by moonlight and see the façade as Longfellow describes it:—

> "Lo! with what depth of blackness thrown
> Against the clouds; far up the skies
> The walls of the Cathedral rise
> Like a mysterious grove of stone.
> The wind is rising; but the boughs
> Rise not and fall not with the wind,
> That through their foliage sobs and soughs;
> Only the cloudy rack behind,
> Drifting onward, wild and ragged,
> Gives to each spire and buttress jagged
> A seeming motion undefined."

After viewing the Cathedral, the Colonel expressed a desire to visit the fortifications. "I cannot show them to you," said Marguérite, "but we have a neighbor, Peter Schnecker, who is a bloodthirsty German, and who will delight in explaining to you all the havoc and destruction which his people inflicted on dear old Strasburg. We will go back by way of his house, and I will ask him to accompany you."

Peter Schnecker happened to be leaning against the palings of his little garden, and the steeple hat took a more defiant

MARGUÉRITE AND PETER SCHNECKER.

angle as Marguérite descried him. He looked very meek and lamb-like, for, though he had never been taught that it is bad manners to retain a cigarette and hat in a lady's company, he was evidently impressed by Marguérite, and dropped his eyes, while his hands fumbled confusedly in his pockets, as if he felt their awkwardness and was anxious to get them out of the way.   He readily agreed to act as our guide for the next day, and we reached the *pension* just in time for dinner.   Here the principal dish was a *paté de foie gras*, for which the city is so famous.   The gentlemen seemed to enjoy it; but the thought of the unnatural way in which the poor geese are crammed to produce their enormous livers quite took away my appetite, and I could not taste a morsel.

Our bedrooms we found chilly and uncomfortable, and we asked Madame Hautcœur if we could not have a fire.   She informed us that a stork had built its nest over the chimney.

"What is to hinder your having it removed?" asked Myrtle.

Madame Hautcœur threw up her hands in horror.   "Ah! who could be so inhuman?" she cried; "besides," she added, in a mysterious whisper, "it would certainly bring misfortune, perhaps death."

MADAME HAUTCŒUR.

And then she told us how, when the city was burning from the shells of the Germans, the storks attempted to coax their young ones from their nests; but, finding that they could not fly, the mother birds cowered down over their fledgelings, protecting them as long as they could from the smoke and flame, and heroically dying with them.

After this we did not care that our rooms were damp and musty. We descended to the cosey sitting-room and spent the evening with the family.   Madame Hautcœur sat in her easy-chair reading, but we prevailed on her to lay aside her book and tell us more about the siege of Strasburg.   I find that it is a great advantage to hear both sides of the affair, and hitherto, it may be, we have championed the German side too unquestioningly.

The French commandant, General Uhrich, certainly exhibited great intrepidity. Before the investment of the city the inhabitants of the surrounding villages flocked in for protection, and the General found himself with over a hundred thousand people to provide for and defend against the clenching German fingers, with only a garrison of disheartened, though brave soldiers, who had already met the enemy and had been defeated in the sanguinary battle of Woerth. "They were gallant men," said Madame; "there were four thousand of the National Guards, and two thousand of the Gardes Mobiles, some *chasseurs* and

STORK'S NEST.

Turcos, and two thousand artillery men; but what were they, with all Germany swarming about us?

"I climbed to the platform of the Cathedral, and the country was black with marching armies as far as the eye could reach.

"The siege began on the 12th of August, and lasted forty days. Ah, it was like the forty days' flood when Noah was in the ark, for it seemed as if 'the great deep was broken up, and the windows of heaven opened'; but the flood was of fire, and the rain was death. The citadel was battered to pieces, fires were burning in a dozen different quarters of Strasburg at once.   Marguérite was at boarding-school; a bomb-shell burst in it, killing seven girls. Do you see that scar on my daughter's cheek? It is where one of the fragments of the shell grazed her, — only a bit of German gallantry.   Those were the kisses which German officers threw to women.   Marguérite fled, terror-stricken and bleeding, through the burning streets to her home.   .

GERMAN SOLDIERS.

"On the 24th, our quarter, the most beautiful in the city, containing the Public Library, one of the richest in Europe, the Art Gallery, the Temple Neuf, and the residences of the aristocracy, was reduced to a heap of blackened ruins. My husband was killed in attempting to extinguish the fire; for whenever the Germans saw a conflagration in any part of the city, they directed their fire to that quarter, to prevent it being suppressed.

"We took refuge in an old house by the river-side, and hid ourselves in the cellar, creeping into the very sewer during the bombardment; but the rains had swollen the Rhine, and the cellars in that part of the town were soon flooded, and we were driven out again.   I called on General Uhrich personally, and it was, I think, in deference to my entreaties that he asked permission of the Germans for the women and children to pass out of the city, a request which was promptly denied. Then, with crowds of other frantic women, we

ANCIENT HOUSES BY THE RIVER.

took refuge in the Cathedral. The good Bishop went out to the German lines, and attempted, without success, to arrange an armistice. The underground telegraphic lines connecting us with Paris were cut by a miner, and all news of what was going on in the outside world was shut out from us until the Germans themselves sent us information of the defeats of Gravelotte and Sedan, of Bazaine shut up in Metz, and the Emperor a prisoner. The 30th of September, the anniversary of the day in 1681 when Strasburg was gained from Germany by Louis XIV., was the day selected for storming the city. But we had suffered enough, and on the 27th General Uhrich commanded the white flag to be hoisted from the topmost spire of the Cathedral. Ah! you should have seen the rage of the French soldiers; those who had served in Africa broke and threw away their arms rather than surrender them. As for me, I was crazed with sorrow, and I cared not whether Strasburg was French or German. Three hundred of my townspeople had been killed, and seventeen hundred wounded, outside of the soldiers, who expect only death, poor fellows, and nearly twenty thousand persons were left homeless and destitute. There were scarcely a hundred houses in the city uninjured. I am French to my heart's core, but, rather than see Strasburg undergo another such siege, I say let her remain German to the end of time."*

We all listened to Madame Hautcœur with the feeling that while war exists we can hardly call ourselves civilized. Even the Colonel had nothing to say in its defence. The next morning, when Peter Schnecker came to guide us over the citadel, we girls were half inclined to remain at home, but, persuaded by the Colonel, we finally joined the party. The citadel was built by Vauban, under Louis XIV., and was supposed to be impregnable. The King caused a medal to be struck off on the taking of the city, with the inscription *Clausa Germanis Gallia* — "France closed to the Germans." Bismarck seems to have had the same idea of its importance, for he called it "the key of the house."

---

* Madame Hautcœur's description is based on Edward King's account of the siege of Strasburg, in his "Europe in Storm and Calm."

I remembered the enthusiasm of Violet le Duc, the French architect for Vauban, and as we viewed the bastions, I tried to remember what he had said of scarp and counterscarp. The Colonel, who is a great admirer of Vauban, considers him the first military architect and engineer of all time. He was a man of immense genius, and, what is better, of sterling honor. He received the bâton of marshal from Louis XIV. after having "directed fifty-three sieges, constructed the fortifications of thirty-three places, and repaired those of three hundred towns"; but in spite of these distinguished services, he was disgraced by his sovereign for daring to present a petition for the recall of the fugitive Huguenots.

This act of Vauban was to me the noblest of his life;

VAUBAN.

aside from it, his work as an engineer, famous as it has made him, does not seem to me the best legacy which a man of his genius could have left his fellow-men. How strange it seems, now that the old castles have become antiquated and useless, that new fortifications and engines of war should take their place. Arbitration between nations seems as much more dignified than war as a legal process between private individuals is more decent than a hand-to-hand fight.

I could not help comparing the two architects Vauban and Erwin von Steinbach, the fortress and the Cathedral: the former, battered and crumbling, passing from the earth like the old reign of violence; the latter, standing through the havoc of war and time, an emblem of the Prince of Peace.

CHAPTER XIV.

THE UPPER RHINE — LAKE CONSTANCE.

HE Tyrol is one of the best localities for the collection of delicate ferns," said a learned looking gentleman with a high bald head, who sat in the same compartment with us in the cars on our way from Strasburg to Constance. "You find the rarest Polypodies there, and the holly fern, which grows half under the snow."

I pricked up my ears; here was a fellow-traveller with kindred tastes, and it was only by a stern contemplation of the conventionalities that I restrained myself from joining in the conversation. I hoped that Joe might introduce us, and explain that I too was a fern fancier, but the remark was addressed to Mr. Blumenthal, and Joe was oblivious, being deeply absorbed in the caricatures of the *Münchner Bilderbogen.* The stranger had a quantity of botanizing paraphernalia with him; a portfolio herbarium and press tightly strapped, some tin boxes, and sponges (in oil silk bags) in which to preserve roots. I watched him with interest, and hoped that a happy chance might make us acquainted, but he left the cars at some little station, and it was not until after he had gone that Mr. Blumenthal informed us that he was a celebrated botanist.

"Why, you ought to have introduced him to Miss Holmes," said Joe, waking up.

"A thousand pardon," replied Mr. Blumenthal, "but ladies generally find him to be dull; he can talk of nothing but the fern. He has just returned himself from the Hawaiian Islands, where he has been for the sole purpose to discover and to collect new varieties. Really, I think I deserve to myself great credit that I have absorb his conversation. He would otherwise have give a lecture to the entire party on the beauties of the *Ophioglossum concimum* and the *Acrosticum Gorgoneum.*"

Mr. Blumenthal looked so happy in the consciousness of having done a good deed that I kept my disappointment to myself, and did not undeceive him.

Myrtle has also met with a disappointment. Just as we left Strasburg, the expected letter arrived from Frau Von Engel. It contained the heartiest of rejoicings, and a cordial welcome into the family. She will be at Munich to meet us, and had telegraphed the happy news to her daughter, the Countess. She had also made thorough investigation, but was sorry to say that no trace could be found of the diamond cross. Heinrich, the gardener, was of the opinion that it had been carried away by ghosts. He had heard a disturbance in the dove-cote on the night that the cross was lost, and had gone out to see what was the matter. The moon shone clearly and he distinctly saw a white-robed lady glide along the balcony in front of our rooms and finally disappear through a window. Frau Von Engel had scoffed at the idea, for the appearance of such a spirit was a very bad omen, but Heinrich had persisted in his story, and it was evident that it had made an impression on the good lady, for she inquired anxiously after Myrtle's health, and hoped that she would be careful not to venture into dangerous places. Myrtle does not give any importance to the apparition, but she is sorry that the cross cannot be found, not so much for its own sake as a proof to her father that she no longer doubts him. It is a mystery which possibly will never be cleared up.

CITY AND CATHEDRAL OF FREIBURG.

We are following the course of the upper Rhine, and passing through the southern portion of the Black Forest. Madame Hautcœur was so kind to us that we felt almost like leaving old friends as the train bore us swiftly away from Strasburg. The Cathedral tower was silhouetted darkly against a brilliant sunset, and I wondered if it had something of the same effect against the burning town during those dreadful nights of siege.

We stopped for the night at the old university town of Freiburg. I made no attempt to obtain instruction here, for the university is one of the last strongholds of Catholicism, and is probably even more conservative than the Protestant universities.

We had made this break in our journey intending to make an excursion by carriage the next day to the Valley of Hell, a narrow gorge or cañon, down which Moreau made his famous retreat in 1796. Moreau was the rival of Napoleon; he gained for the French the battle of Hohenlinden, and he saved his army from being cut off by a retreat which was so skilfully managed that it was equivalent to a victory. But we were not destined to see the Höllenpass, for in the morning the rain descended in torrents. We took the train again, and passing Basle, which looked forlorn and uninviting through the veil of rain, paused next at Schaffhausen, just as the storm cleared away. The picturesque market-place was washed clean by the rain, and, freshly gilded by the sunshine, had a beautiful effect.

We heard some fine singing here in the evening; selections from the " Freischütz," by amateurs. The legend of the Freeshooter probably originated in this vicinity, which is a great hunting region. Huntsmen even now, if they are so fortunate as to hit their mark six times in succession in one day, will not fire for a seventh time, for fear that the devil will direct the ball as he pleases. It surprised me to find what beautiful voices these sturdy highlanders have. All the musicians that I happened to know at home were frail, ethereal beings, their higher natures developed at the expense of the lower, while the

Germans seem to combine the real with the ideal more closely than any other nation. I mentioned this to Mr. Blumenthal, and he quoted from Auerbach: —

"Oh beautiful, glorious Germany! This is life! This is our life to build up the soul with song, and the body with lusty motion; this makes a people strong and beautiful. Everything glorious belongs to us as fully as it did to the classical world."

We have visited the Cathedral, and have seen the great bell, cast in 1484, which bears the inscription: —

PEASANT KNITTING.

Vivos voco.	I call the living.
Mortuos plango.	I mourn the dead.
Fulgura frango.	I break the lightnings.

This inscription is said to have given Schiller the idea of his Lied von der Glocke. Longfellow also makes use of it.

We drove out to see the falls of Schaffhausen, two miles lower down the Rhine. The city owes its original name, Schiffhäusen, to the warehouses built here to protect the goods unloaded from the boats, which could go no farther down, on account of the falls and rapids. Schloss Laufen, above the falls, is the spot from which ladies usually view the cataract, but we insisted on going out on the Fischetz, a long wooden gallery just below, when we were stunned by the noise and blinded by the spray. An old woman who was watching some sheep, and at the same time knitting a coarse woollen stocking, told us that salmon were caught below the falls and trout above. On our return to Schaffhausen, we visited the Castle of

THE VALLEY OF HELL.

Unnoth, which is strongly fortified. Its walls rise directly from the river, which is overhung by its queer balconies and oriels. It is said that it was designed by the painter Albert Dürer; that it is provided with bomb-proof casemates, and that its walls are eighteen feet thick, but I fear that it would stand a modern siege no better than Vauban's citadel at Strasburg.

CONSTANCE.

Both lake and town are very interesting; but the lake, or Bodensee, as the natives call it, interested me most. We have taken several trips upon it in the little steamer which plies on its dark green waters. The Rhine runs through Lake Constance; the lake may even be considered, like the Rheingau, as simply an enlargement of the river. We are never tired of looking down into the water, — hunting for nixies, Joe says. And, indeed, it seems to us that this would be the best place to locate the scene of the Rheingold from Wagner's Nibelung drama.

Miss Boylston sang snatches from the frolics of the river nymphs, as they tease the adventurous mortal who has ventured into their element to steal the precious gold which they are set to guard.

> " The wealth of the world
>   To him we will fling,
> Who from the Rhinegold,
>   Hammers a ring.
>
> " Who from delight
>   His heart can withhold.
> Who in the light
>   Of love is cold,
> Whom no bribe can decoy, or charm can lure,
>   He shall possess the Rhinegold pure."

" Then it's yours, my dear," Myrtle said, as Miss Boylston sang this. "If the rest of us could only possess your calm unimpressionableness, temptations would rebound from our hearts like a shower of pebbles from armor of proof."

Miss Boylston smiled gravely.   "Unimpressionableness is a long word," she said, "and it takes almost as long to acquire it as to spell it."

Miss Boylston is really an old maid; I wondered whether there were not some story locked behind her impassive demeanor, and one day when we were rambling among the lower ranges of Alps on the south of the lake, and we were separated for a time from the rest of the party, I asked her. "No," she replied, quite simply, "there is no love story in my life. I do not undervalue Myrtle's happiness. It must make a woman very humble as well as proud to be honored by a good man's love. It is one of the blessings which have never come to me, but my life has been so full that I have not

HÔTEL DE VILLE, ULM.

missed it. I do not see how any one can be unhappy with work to do — such work as mine, I mean, to which one can give one's whole

MARKET-PLACE AT SCHAFFHAUSEN.

soul." We had not noticed that a passing shower was driving swiftly in our direction. It overtook us just as we were most absorbed. Fortunately there was a goatherd's hut near by, and into it we crept, the goatherd obligingly going out into the rain to make us room. He spoke a queer Swiss patois, and promised to show us some edelweiss after the shower. The others came up after a time; they had been protected by waterproofs, and laughed at the rain and at our queer shelter; we picnicked in front of the hut, and shared our luncheon with the goatherd, who, in return, gave us fresh goat's-milk, which he milked into Myrtle's silver mug.

At the hotels in this region we have been served to chamois, partridges, hares, venison, and delicious trout. The gentlemen of our party have been wild to get a shot at real live chamois, and to catch a few trout. They have been on repeated hunting and fishing excursions without the slightest success. They even secured the little goatherd as guide, but the chamois seemed to fly before them. They fancied that they had seen one on a lofty crag, but Mr. Blumenthal was of the opinion that it was only an adventurous goat, and that for real chamois one must go higher up into the Alps. On their return from an unsuccessful fishing excursion, Myrtle greeted them with the following jingle, which was loudly applauded: —

How doth the little speckled trout
Improve each shining hour,
And all the students' efforts flout
To coax them to their power.

How skilfully they snap the fly
And leave the naked hook.
They make the maidens grieve and sigh,
And disappoint the cook.

If wives were caught with rod and reel,
They'd cheat their fishers too.
For Satan finds some mischief still
For trout and girls to do!

Joe has purchased for himself a handsome alpenstock, tipped with the small black horn of a chamois. It is the fashion for Alpine tourists to have these staves ornamented with the carved names of the mountain-peaks which they have ascended. We saw one literally

BAVARIAN SKETCHES.

covered with names of the highest mountains, which made us a little suspicious of the veracity of its owner. Joe, not to be outdone, has cut on his the loftiest peaks of the Andes, Chimborazo, Cotopaxi, etc., with Mt. Everest and Kunchain-Junga in the Himalayas.

We have crossed the lake for the last time, and are now on our way to Munich, *via* the ancient city of Augsburg, so associated with the Reformation, with Charles V., with the paintings of Holbein, the merchant princes of the house of Fugger, and with beautiful old carvings and iron-work. The old Gothic city of Ulm is also on our route, and the Bavarian human types are, if possible, more intensely German than those of the Rhine. This part of Bavaria is full of ruined castles. Two hundred and eighty of such ruins have been counted. There were turns in the road where we could see five at a time. I had been praising the scenery of America, and had lamented that we had no ruined castles, for in every

THE GOATHERD'S HUT.

other respect the Hudson would compare favorably with the Rhine.

"You know Goethe thought you were better off without them," Mr. Blumenthal remarked.

"I did not know that Goethe ever interested himself in America," I replied, and Mr. Blumenthal, turning to his note-book, read: —

> "America, du hast es besser
> Als unser Continent, das alte ;
> Hast keine verfallene Schlösser,
> Und keine Basalte.
> Dich stört nicht im Innern,
> Zu lebendiger Zeit,
> Unnützes Erinnern
> Und vergeblicher Streit.
> Benützt die Gegenwart mit Glück !
> Und wenn nun Eure Kinder dichten,
> Bewahre sie ein gut Geshick
> Vor Ritter, Raüber, und Gespenstergeschichten." *

* Translation: "America, thou art more fortunate than our continent, the old. Thou hast no ruined castles and pillars. In thy living age, no useless memories and vain struggles weigh upon thee. Use the present wisely, and when thy children shall sing of thee, may good destiny preserve them from legends of knights, robbers, and ghosts."

CHAPTER XV.

MUNICH.

IN A REAL PALACE.

A ND this is Munich; I sit in a real palace, a tiny one to be sure, but still a building which, in its time, has been a veritable princely "*Residenz*," and has been fitted up most charmingly by the Countess, with antique furniture and bric-à-brac. The best of it is that this furniture has not been bought at Sypher's, but has been handed down from generation to generation, for the Count's family is a very ancient one. This ormolu cabinet is part of a set given to his great grandfather by Frederick the Great. Here is a vase that, for aught I know, may date from Charlemagne. Those gilt sconces are of the time of Louis XIV., but they are a recent acquisition, for all that, for the Count brought them back from Paris on his return from the little military excursion which ended so disastrously for the French. There are paintings by Dürer and Holbein, and gems which have glistened on the throats of princesses; but the greatest treasures which the house holds are, to my mind, the Countess' lovely children.

Adolf is a beautiful, serious boy, with the eyes of a poet; his sister, who rejoices in the stately name of Amalie Bertha Charlotte Clau-

ADOLF.

dine, is a tricksy little sprite, with such very light hair that her uncle has nicknamed her *Weissmäuschen,* or the little white mouse, and so the rest of us call her. Frau Von Engel and her eldest son are here with quite a retinue, and an apparently interminable programme of festivities has been arranged to celebrate, not the betrothal of Myrtle and Mr. Blumenthal, but their marriage, for the Von Engels brought forward so many good reasons why this should be, that Myrtle and her father have consented.

The young couple are to live in Munich, and Mr. Blumenthal will finish his art studies with Piloty, who, since the death of Kaulbach, is the leading German figure-painter.

The family are so busy with preparations for the wedding, that Miss Boylston and I have begged them not to treat us as guests who need entertainment, but have instituted a series of rambles about the city for our own diversion. The Countess has placed a coupé with liveried driver at our service, and we enjoy our jaunts exceedingly. The Ludwig-Strasse is one of our favorite drives, with its beautiful Siegesthor or Triumphal Arch. It is built of glistening Carrara marble, and surmounted by a noble group in

WEISSMÄUSCHEN.

bronze, Bavaria, seated in a chariot drawn by lions. This must not be confused with the colossal statue of Bavaria, that stands in front of the Hall of Fame, which contains the busts of celebrated Bavarians. The great Bavaria is seventy feet high; it is hollow, and a staircase leads to the neck, from which point we climbed up an iron ladder into the head, and obtained a fine view of the city. It

TRIUMPHAL ARCH, MUNICH.

was a warm day, and the sun had heated the bronze so that we could scarcely bear to touch it. We felt as if we were shut up in the burning fiery furnace of Shadrach, Meshach, and Abednego, or in one of the statues in which the victims to Moloch were roasted alive. The air was stifling; mounting so many stairs had made me quite giddy, and it was all that I could do to scramble down again.

CASTLE OF UNNOTH.

One afternoon Mr. Blumenthal, whom we must now accustom ourselves to call Herr Von Engel, took us to visit the studios of the noted modern artists of the Munich school. As a general thing, although some of them are very handsome, they are situated in back

STATUE OF BAVARIA.

yards and are approached by queer little *strassen* and courts. We ring a bell at a gate and are admitted by a portress into a garden. I have not time to describe all that I saw, and can only make a note or two to recall to my mind a series of charming visits. Piloty is an exceedingly broad man (I do not mean in physical proportions). He is best known to Americans by his historical paintings, especially the grand " Germanicus before Cæsar." We saw some sketches and studies for this work.

We were also greatly interested in the pictures of Herr Dietz, of whom I had never heard; he delights in the representation of horses and the old robbers who once inhabited the ruined castles of this region.

We had a charming visit at Wagner's studio. He also enjoys horses. He seemed pleased when I told him how much his " Chariot Race" was admired, and how widely it had been reproduced, in America. He is a Hungarian, and all of his pictures have a dash and go which are exhilarating to behold. He showed us a " Hungarian Turf Race," where the horses seemed to be prancing out of the canvas. He has decorated the Munich Museum with scenes from the Thirty Years' War.

Defregger, whose paintings of peasants I have already mentioned, has a studio in Munich. Loefts ought to be better known with us for his scriptural subjects, executed in the style of Holbein, of whom he is a passionate admirer. I was introduced to Professor Raub, who teaches engraving in the Munich Academy; he told me that he had taught many Americans, and that they were all bright men. Linden Schmidt is another of the notable painters of this art-loving city. I remember seeing his portrait of Luther in New York before we sailed.

I heard many anecdotes of Kaulbach, the great master, who has passed away. He was a genial little man, fond of a quiet joke, modest and unobtrusive, though painting in the grandest way. I had known him only through a set of photographs, the heroines of Schiller and Goethe. We went to see his cartoons on the outside of the new Pinacothek, — which are unhappily rapidly fading, from the effect of the weather, — and another set, in what is called the " English Garden," a charming spot near the royal palace, which belonged to Count Rumford, the scientist. Here the paintings are protected by arcades, and are in a better state of preservation. The Pinacothek is said to be one of the richest of European picture-galleries. We have spent hours studying its masterpieces. The Glyptothek, or Gallery of Sculpture, has many beautiful specimens of Greek art. One, a "Sleeping Faun" is said to have been hurled at the invading Goths as a projectile from the Castle of St. Angelo.

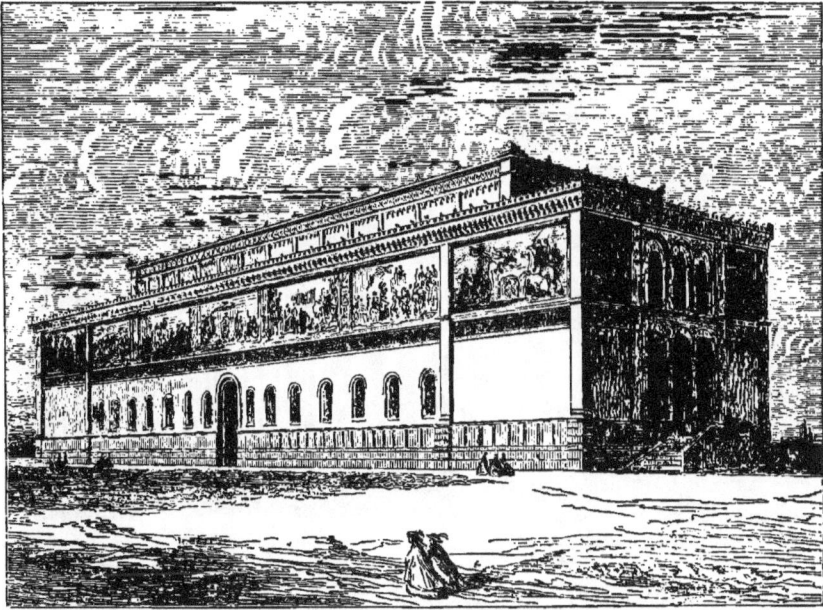

THE PINACOTHEK.

The Countess has taken us to a court reception at the new Residenz. We were presented to the Princess. I think I hardly enjoyed the occasion, splendid as it was, so much as a visit which I made with little Adolf, through the kindness of the marshal of the household, to the royal stables.

Here we saw horses spirited enough to have pleased Herr Wagner, and one of the grooms removed the covers from the sledges in which the king of Bavaria and his suite enjoy sleighing parties in the Bavarian Alps.   Some of them were enormous, covered with gilding and carved figures, holding the crown-shaped canopies.   One was in the form of a shell supported by Tritons and Cupids, and others had their

THE GLYPTOTHEK.

panels decorated by the best artists.   Adolf had taken part in one of the sleighing parties; he described the flashing lights, the shadows following like the spectral erl-king over the snow.   Each sledge had its cornet-player, who wound his horn at intervals and set the wild echoes flying.

Adolf and I are great friends.   Half of the carved toys which I purchased in the Black Forest for American children have found their way to him and to his little sister.

The Count, in spite of his ferocious whiskers, is very harmless. More than this, he is most kind and thoughtful. Learning of my vain quest for instruction, he has written to the great specialist, Professor Schwendeuer of Berlin, and has obtained for me admission to his classes. Frau Von Engel has friends in Berlin who have agreed to take me into their family, so all that is happily settled, and I am to begin my studies immediately after the wedding.

The festivities have begun with a ball. The greater part of the gentlemen were officers; they entered the room with their helmets under their arms, and their swords buckled about them. These adornments were laid aside, however, before the dancing began. The german is danced here quite differently from the manner in which we had been

UNCLE KALBFLEISCH.

instructed. A little kiosk was trundled into the middle of the ballroom. It was labelled "Office for the sale of Lottery Tickets." The ladies were informed that they were the prizes, and we each received paper decorations. Mine was a cap of silver tissue, shaped like a beer tankard. Myrtle had an enormous necklace of paste gems; Miss Boylston a huge tissue paper bouquet, and so forth. Then the gentlemen received their tickets which allowed them to dance with the prize they had drawn.

Sometimes, we were told, very large set pieces are introduced, elephants and giraffes, or other zoölogical curiosities. For perfect *abandon* and heartiness there is no fun like German fun.

The wedding presents have begun to arrive; some of them very expensive, others again are most practical.   They range all the way from a gold tea-service and set of pearls, presented by a Crown Prin cess and a Grand Duke, to a receipted bill for the plumbing of the new home, from a friend in that business, and a fine cow from Uncle Kalbfleisch.   Frau Von Engel presented the house-linen, all carefully marked by her own hand.   The Colonel has given his daughter an ample allowance, which, whatever the income of the young artist, will suffice to keep the wolf from the door.   Miss Boylston and I have helped arrange the furniture in the pretty suite of apartments. We have hung the dainty muslin curtains, and just over Myrtle's desk I have placed a cabinet bookcase, with a few choice books by American authors, so that she may not forget her native land.

Miss Boylston's present is a fine music-box, which she purchased in the Black Forest, which plays some of her favorite tunes.

Joe has given his sister an elegantly bound *cook-book*.   On the blank leaf he has copied a rhyming skit from one of the American newspapers: —

She'd a great and varied knowledge, absorbed at Vassar College, of quadratics, hydro-
  statics, and pneumatics very vast.

She was stuffed with erudition as you stuff a leather cushion, all the ologies of the col-
  leges and the knowledges of the past.

She had studied the old lexicons of Peruvians and Mexicans, their theology, anthro-
  pology, and geology, o'er and o'er.

She knew all the forms and features of the pre-historic creatures — icythyosaurus,
  plesiosaurus, megalosaurus, and many more.

She'd describe the ancient Tuscans, and the Basques and the Etruscans, their griddles
  and their kettles and the victuals that they gnawed.

She'd discuss — the learned charmer — the theology of Bramah, and the scandals of
  the Vandals, and the sandals that they trod.

She knew all the mighty giants and the master minds of science, all the learning that
was turning in the burning mind of man.

But she couldn't prepare a dinner for a gaunt and hungry sinner, or get up a decent
supper for her poor voracious papa, for she never was constructed on the old
domestic plan.

It is all a libel. Myrtle is really inclined to be very domestic, and
will easily learn the thrifty German ways. She has already learned
how to make Goethe's favorite pudding, the Charlotte, a complicated
affair of blanched almonds, grated chocolate, crushed macaroons,
rose-water, and I know not what. I think that her ambition was
stirred, not from the fact that the great author was fond of it, but
because Frau Von Engel remarked that any one who could achieve
a Charlotte pudding was equal to anything else in the line of cooking.
Myrtle made friends with the Countess' chef, made the pudding, and
when it appeared was rewarded by hearing Frau Von Engel compliment her daughter on her very superior cook. Little Weissmäuschen
is troubled because she has no present for Myrtle, and her mother is
so absorbed that she has not time to pay attention to the child's fancy.
I told her that Myrtle would be more pleased with a few flowers
from the garden than with a more costly present from a stranger.

The wedding is over, and with it a train of attendant circumstances
enough to make the steadiest brain whirl. First, the legal settlements in regard to property, then the arrival of Myrtle's trousseau
from Paris, only a few dresses, but all beautifully made and in the
best of taste. I was her only bridesmaid, for Miss Boylston officiated
at the organ. The wedding proper was at the English chapel, which
was beautifully decorated. The Episcopal ceremony never seemed
to me more impressive. Myrtle was calm and sweetly dignified.
How very certain one must be of one's own heart to take those
solemn vows! but there was an infinite trust and confidence in her

face, and a grave sincerity in that of the bridegroom, which spoke well for their future happiness.

Beside the ceremony at the church, there is also in Germany a civil marriage, which must be performed. An old gentleman read the legal forms and then discoursed solemnly on the responsibilities of matrimony, ending with a beautiful poem. I had expected that this part of the ceremony would be very dry, but, to my surprise, my eyes were wet. It is only another instance of the way in which the Germans blend the practical and the ideal. After the marriage ceremony there was a wedding breakfast, and then the bride and groom left us for a tour through Switzerland.

While we were at table, we heard a light crash on the pavement just outside. "Some one has knocked your tulip from the window," said Joe. "How thankful your husband ought to be, now that detestable flower-pot will not have to be carried over all the Swiss glaciers." Weissmäuschen scrambled from her seat, curious to see what was broken, and she did not make her appearance until the moment of departure. Then, just as Myrtle was entering the carriage, the child came down the steps, holding in her hand a fragment of the broken flower-pot. "Stop," she cried, "I have a present for my little Aunt." Myrtle came back and uttered a low cry of delight, as the child handed her, caked with earth, and entwined by roots, the lost diamond cross!

"Your present is best of all," Myrtle exclaimed, and then every one fell to chattering, asking questions, and trying to explain its presence in the flower-pot. "The thief must have secreted it there," said Joe, "and long ago, for see how the tulip-roots have grown around it."

"It is the work of the ghost, the white lady," exclaimed Frau Von Engel.

"You are both right," said Miss Boylston; "but, Myrtle dear, you were yourself burglar and spectre!"

" I!" replied Myrtle, in surprise.

"Not consciously, of course; but do you not remember the sleep-walking at Oberkirch, and how you pulled up Dortchen's poor posies?"

"I must have recurred to the idea of my first somnambulistic feat," said Myrtle, in a dazed way. "How strange that we forget when we wake, and remember again when we dream!"

"Come," said Mr. Blumenthal, "we will certainly lose the train."

The Colonel embraced his daughter with a triumphant happiness shining in his moist eyes. "I shall have to apologize to Mr. Van Bergen," was all he said.

The Colonel is really going to carry out his intention of entering the German army. Myrtle and he are completely de-Americanized. Not so Joe; he will return to Louisiana, to do what he can with the paternal estate, and will then carve a future for himself in our own dear country. Miss Boylston, too, sails for America soon. She is absorbed in her mission, and as calmly happy, I really believe, as

A GIFT FOR THE BRIDE.

Myrtle in her different life. They represent the colors of our Alma Mater, the rose and silver-gray. I wonder which is best? If it were only possible to braid the tints, and combine a high intellectual career with a happy home-life! But this is idle dreaming, and my beloved ferns are waiting for me at Berlin. Will any three girls ever pass a pleasanter summer than ours upon the Rhine?

CHAPTER XVI.

NUREMBERG. — GRIEF AND JOY.

DELIGHT HOLMES' journal of the doings and happenings of Three Vassar Girls on the Rhine ended here. In her student-days which followed in Berlin, she was at first too busy to write of her experiences, interesting though they were, except in her weekly letters to her parents. But there came a day when she found leisure, the sad leisure which comes to us when the object of all our toil is suddenly removed, and all our ambition and aspiration are suddenly dashed to the ground.

Word came to her that her father, whom she idolized, the old Professor for whose sake she had sought to become a learned special-ist, who had taken so much pride in her acquirements, and who loved her so fondly, had gone to the Source of the Nature which he loved.

"You need not come home on this account," her mother had written. "I shall live with your older brother, and you can still devote yourself to your chosen career."

Delight had never realized before how her father had been the mainspring of all her actions. Her chosen career had always been to please him. She would not have gone abroad but for this. Her only ambition was that her success might make him happy. Miss Boylston was self-poised, so rapt in her devotion to music, and in her hope of making the music of some church truly devotional in its character, that she forgot every one else, and even herself, in her noble purpose; but Delight was more affectionate in her nature. She had worked, and would always labor, not so much for her own gratification, or for any abstract end, as for directly helping some one whom she loved. Now it seemed to her as if she could not live on, and study alone, and her life stretched before her dreary and aimless.

"If I had chosen some work that would more directly benefit my fellow-creatures," she said to herself, "then I might live on for its sake, but I interested myself in what father cared for, and now there is no longer any need in my living."

She would go back to America, she decided, and she found time, in the fortnight before she sailed for home, to dream for a little while of the past and the future, and to wonder what relation they might bear each other.

While pursuing her scientific studies in Berlin, she had fol-

THE BRIDE'S DOOR, NUREMBERG.

lowed eagerly every tradition in regard to Alexander Von Humboldt.

She had been specially interested in him at first at Vassar, from hearing Professor Maria Mitchell tell of her interview with him, and, secondly, from having followed, with her father, a part of his wanderings among the Andes; but she could not remember the time when his name was not a household word, and his works were the most thoroughly thumbed of any in her father's library.

Humboldt had lived in Berlin. She visited the rooms where Bayard Taylor called upon him, and saw his collection of stuffed birds and his library. He had been a professor in the University with Neander, Schleiermacher, Schelling, Ritter, and the other celebrated men. The old gentleman at whose house she boarded had once been a student of the University, and had attended Humboldt's lectures. He hunted up a little book, yellow with age, and read her the notes which he had made in the class-room. These familiar talks of Humboldt with his students had never been published, or even written out by their author. There was one, a description of the sea-weed of the Pacific coast of South America, which greatly interested Delight, as she had made collections with her father from the same waters. Her friend allowed her to translate the notes, and expressed his entire willingness for her to use them in any way she pleased. She had planned to publish them on her return to America, supplemented by the later observations and discoveries of her father, and she had often pictured to herself the pleasure he would have, if alive, in aiding her in the preparation of this work.

She had improved her stay in Berlin not alone in research in exact science, but had studied German literature, through readings with the family with whom she boarded, from Goethe, Schiller, Jean Paul, Schlegel, Novalis, Uhland, Heine, and Grimm. But, with all her earnestness, she was often lonely, and with the coming of this springtime a mighty wave of homesickness and longing lifted her on its irresistible, dizzy swell. She determined to run down to Munich for a few days and ease her heart with Myrtle before she embarked on that other lonely ocean, to meet she knew not what.

But Myrtle, her husband, and the Countess had all left Munich only the day before. Only Weissmäuschen was trundling her dolls in the garden, and dropped her small family in happy surprise at seeing Delight. The child's prattle was a brief pleasure. She took De-light to see the doll of the cook's little girl. The cook had been in New York and had brought back this doll, which he said was a full-blooded American, but Weissmäuschen had disputed the fact, asserting that she had known several Americans, and this doll was only a woolly-headed African, its hair con-structed from a woollen stocking. She wanted Delight to refute the libel, and to prove that Americans were not black. Delight chatted a few moments with the children, and then took the train again, sadder, if possible, for her visit. The servants could not tell her where her friends had gone. Miss Boylston had returned to America, and in all Europe there seemed to be no one to sympathize with her in her trouble. She found the trains so arranged that it would be more convenient to stop for the night in Nuremberg than to go on, and as she had been recommended by her Berlin friends to a quiet family in this city who kept boarders, she availed herself of the opportunity for visiting the

WEISSMÄUSCHEN AND HER FAMILY.

"Quaint old town of toil and traffic, quaint old town of art and song."

She found a landlady with a kindly heart set in a capacious bosom. Something in Delight's sad face touched her sympathies, and she set out her bountiful table with even more abundance than usual. "When the sad eat," she said to herself, "they are cheered in spite

of themselves, and that is the reason we always have a feast after a funeral."

The landlady's husband asked Delight if she had ever read Heine's gibe at German cookery. "He was always ridiculing our officers and our fare."

At Delight's request he repeated the poem: —

AN AMERICAN DOLL.

The table was spread, and here I found
The real old German cooking.
I greet thee dear old sauer-kraut,
With thy delicate perfume smoking.

Mother's stuffed chestnuts in cabbage green,
They set my heart in a flutter;
Codfish of my country, I greet ye fine,
As ye cunningly swim in your butter.

How the sausages swelled in sputtering fat,
And field-fares, small angels pious,
All roasted and swaddled in apple sauce,
Twittered out to me, "Try us!"

A goose, a quiet and genial soul,
Was on the table extended;
Perhaps she loved me once, in the days
Before our youth was ended.

She threw at me such a meaning look,
So trustful, tender, and pensive;
Her soul was beautiful, but her meat —
Was tough, I'm apprehensive.

On a pewter plate a pig's head they brought;
And you know, in the German nation,
It's the snouts of the pigs they always select
For a laurel decoration.

NUREMBERG MARKET-PLACE.

But the girl's heart was too sore for her to even force a smile, and the well-meaning man concluded that he must have made a blunder, that Delight had military friends, and resented the insinuation at the close of the poem.

The landlady proposed that her daughter Katchen should show Delight the points of interest on the morrow. She gratefully assented, and, retiring to the neat little chamber, tried to shut out the sad thoughts which were numbing heart and brain, by telling over to herself all she had read and heard of Nuremberg. Again she was sure that Longfellow had best summed up its attractions: —

> In the valley of the Pegnitz, where across broad meadow lands
> Rise the blue Franconian mountains, Nuremberg the ancient stands.
>
> Everywhere I see around me rise the wondrous world of Art;
> Fountains wrought with richest sculpture standing in the common mart.
>
> In the church of sainted Lawrence stands a pix of sculpture rare,
> Like the foamy sheaf of fountains rising through the painted air.
>
> Here, when Art was still religion, with a simple, reverent heart,
> Lived and labored Albrecht Dürer, the Evangelist of Art.
>
> Here Hans Sachs, the cobbler-poet, laureate of the gentle craft,
> Wisest of the Twelve Wise Masters, in huge folios sang and laughed.
>
> But his house is now an ale-house, with a nicely sanded floor,
> And a garland in the window, and his face above the door.
>
> Not thy Councils, not thy Kaisers, win for thee the world's regard;
> But thy painter, Albrecht Dürer, and Hans Sachs, thy cobbler-bard.

Even with this foretelling of what was to come, when the morning came, Delight was in no mood for sight-seeing, but she had a conscientious feeling that she might some day regret it if she turned her back on the masterpieces of art which have made the city famous. Her landlady's daughter, a black-eyed girl, stood holding her round

hat, waiting to show her about the town, and she choked back the
lump in her throat, roused herself from her melancholy, and followed
her guide out into the sunshine. She had no thought of diversion,
but the moment that she stepped outside the house and wandered
down the crooked streets overhung with pointed gables and sharply
peaked roofs, it seemed to her that she had gone away from herself,
and was walking somewhere in the 17th century. Here was Albert
Dürer's house, looking homelike and no older than its
neighbors, and here was the home of Hans Sachs, the
cobbler-poet.   It seemed to her that she might meet
either of them at the turn of the next corner.   She
stood long before the Beautiful Fountain, with its forest
of hammered iron tracery flaming up into Gothic pinnacles, and curling into tendrils and leafage, until it
seemed as if the iron had blossomed.   They visited
the church of St. Sebald, and later she strayed into the
church of St. Lorenz.   Here she followed her guide
from altar to altar, but when she reached the wonderful pyx of Adam Kraft,—a casket chiselled from
white sandstone to contain the sacrament, — she sent
away the talkative girl.   "I would rather stay and
study it alone," she said, and, sitting alone in the solemn
building with this wonder of beauty before her, she

THE LANDLADY'S
DAUGHTER.

felt that good Adam Kraft, as he labored, must have
really believed that he was building a shrine for the Divine Presence, a house which Christ would truly inhabit, and for a time she
forgot her own sorrow in the contemplation of this marvellous result
of his great patience. Bayard Taylor has best described this beautiful work, and I quote his description: —

"This pyx stands beside one of the pillars of the chancel, and
spires upward, like a fountain, under the arch, to the height of more
than sixty feet. The house containing the vessels is imbedded in an

arbor of vines, forming
leafy grottos, with
niches in which stand
statues of the Apostles.
The Gothic pinnacles,
which shoot up through
this canopy of foliage,
bud into leafy orna-
ments at their tops, and
bend over and wave
downwards like vines
swinging in the air.
Upwards, still dimin-
ishing, rises the airy
tracery of the spire,
with spray-like needles
leaping from every
angle, till at the sum-
mit the frail stem
curves like a flower-
stalk, and hangs in the
air a last tendril over
the wonderful arbor
out of which it grew.
Grand Adam Kraft!
glorious old master!
God grant that this
beautiful creation some-
times consoled the bit-
terness of thy desti-
tute and neglected old
age."

THE CHOIR OF ST. SEBALD.

Bayard Taylor tells us further how Kraft, "with his apprentice and journeyman, made it in five years, and received therefor not quite three hundred dollars; how the people had no faith in his work, but believed he had a secret method of softening stone and casting it into moulds; and how it was afterward proved to be really chiselled."

A great calm came into Delight's soul. If this man could labor on through misapprehension and scorn, with none to appreciate or sympathize, could not she also struggle to make of herself a sacred pyx, a shrine for the Lord, in which he would condescend to dwell. She was lifted above her loneliness with the sense of divine companionship. Christ would come and live within her, and she would never more be alone. She would go on with her study, for it was worthy work, and if her father could know of her life, he would be glad that she was so occupied, but she would not grieve for him rebelliously, or feel herself desolate and deserted. The Roman Catholic dogma of the Real Presence was true in this higher sense. Christ might not be in the consecrated wafer within the beautiful pyx, but he, who,

> "Within no walls confined,
> Inhabiteth the humble mind,"

would dwell with her and within her, making the temple worthy of his presence.

It was a day never to be forgotten, and she went back to Berlin, ready to take up the burden of life again bravely and cheerfully, because trustfully. She found, too, that she was not so forsaken of all human comfort as she had supposed. Before leaving Nuremberg, she visited the old castle which crowns a precipice overhanging the city. The beautiful panorama of picturesque roofs stretched from her feet away to the misty mountains. The castle moat lay far below her feet, and the walls, massive and high, towered around her. A little poem of Klaus Groth's came to her mind, and she sang the first

RAMPARTS OF NUREMBERG.

verse, believing herself to be quite alone, for the landlady's daughter had stopped to gossip with the janitress: —

> "No ditch is so deep, and no wall is so high,
> If two love each other, they'll meet by and by."

What a false little jingle it was! There was some one whom she loved, and who, she had fancied, loved her, but a wall of distance as impenetrable as these granite blocks, and a gulf of misunderstanding as deep as the moat, separated them. But even as this thought passed through her mind, a voice below her caught up the melody, and answered: —

> "There is surely a ladder, a step, or a stile.
> If two love each other, they'll meet ere long while."

It was Joe who came leaping up the narrow path, and in the next instant was listening to all the sad story of her grief and the miracle of consolation which had come to her in the old church.

Joe listened reverently. "Myrtle wrote me of your father's death," Joe said. "Here is her letter. 'Now is the time,' she writes, 'for her friends to fly to her assistance. We leave for Berlin this afternoon.'"

"Then Myrtle and I must have crossed each other," Delight said, "and she is probably in Berlin, waiting for me."

"Yes, and I came too, but when half way my heart failed, and I turned off to see Nuremberg. It seemed to me that you could never care for my comfort, and that, at a time like this, my presence would be an intrusion."

What Delight replied we need not tell. The greatest joy of her life came to her, consecrated by her grief, and Joe himself was sobered and changed by the experience. It was no slight thing to offer himself as in some sort a substitute for the faithful father, a sup-porter and protector of this loving, trusting girl. But his soul expanded with the thought. Please God, he would not prove a broken reed, and his life, too, should be a consecration. They joined the Boujoulacs, and a little later another and a quieter wedding was celebrated, followed by a remarkable wedding-tour. Through the influence of the Count, the young couple were invited to join an expedition for deep-sea soundings in Southern seas. Joe was given employment in mechanical parts of the service, for which his education had fitted him, and Delight would have the classifying of the sea-weed brought up by the steam-dredger.

Her father's field of observation, and even Humboldt's, was meagre compared to the one which now stretched before her. There was another scientific lady, the wife of the Captain, in the party, who would be glad of her company. It seemed to her too good to be true; her mother sent a cheerful sanction; if only her father could have lived to see her life so doubly crowned with love and opportunity, the best of life!

"The best of life, did you say?" said Professor Hammer, the old Kapellmeister, "well, perhaps, for your age, you estimate it right. It makes a difference at what time of life we consider that question."

Later, Professor Hammer wrote a little poem, which he handed Delight. It ran as follows: —

WHAT'S BEST IN LIFE?

What's best in life, gay-hearted girl?
Why, beauty, youth, this ring and pearl,
Which tell of some one's love for me,
And love I'm sure all must agree
    Is best of life.

What's best of life, O busy brain?
The sense of power to strive and gain;
And Inspiration's joyous thrill,
And work a balm for every ill,
    Work's best in life.

What's best in life, wise heart and true?
We learn it late — the good we do;
Old wrongs made right, hearts healed that break,
The unknown act for Christ's dear sake,
      Are best of life.

What's best in life, () silver hair?
You've tasted all its joy and care,
Is 't work for others or for self,
Or love or fame, or mirth or pelf,
      What's best in life?

The happiest hour of all the day
Is when you press your couch, and say,
Work's done, now welcome rest, good night,
So Death, who kindly shuts the light,
      Is best of life.

Was it a strange marriage poem? Death and Love had come to Delight hand in hand, and in our mingled life they are never far separated. Happiest are they who in their day of joy can calmly contemplate dark days, knowing that Divine Love, once invited as guest, will never leave them nor forsake them, and, though the beginning be bright, more glorious will be —

THE END.